CREATING A LIFE
YOU LOVE

1001 INTENTIONS

SWAMI SHANKARANANDA GIRI

CREATING A LIFE
YOU LOVE

IOOI INTENTIONS

SWAMI SHANKARANANDA GIRI

EDITED BY SRIMATI SHANTI MATAJI

DARSHAN

BALTIMORE, MD

CREATING A LIFE YOU LOVE:
1001 INTENTIONS

Cover photographs: Shambu (Bill Tipper)
Design: Anna Berkheiser
Compiled by: Shraddha (Lucy Hagan)

AUM

To my fellow devotees at Divine Life Church,
Thank you for inspiring me to create these noble intentions
to benefit everyone who is guided to apply them.

With profound love and gratitude of Soul,
Swami Shankarananda

CONTENTS

PART TWO: 1001 INTENTIONS

FOREWORD

We are all immensely creative—not just those who are
artists or poets. We are all creating every moment of every
day with our thoughts, positive or negative; with our worries
and our fears; with our patterns of expectations and things
we want to avoid; in fact, with every desire to have something
or, just as powerfully, with desires not to have something.

In most of us, our thoughts jumble together, and we are
sending mixed messages to the universe, unless we have
disciplined the mind to hold to the thoughts that help us
create what we truly want in life. Intentions are a powerful
way to focus our thoughts and emotions in a positive, loving
direction. We know that a piece of iron, just a common
iron bar, does not have the power to pick up another piece
of metal. But when you rub the iron bar with a magnet, the
plain iron bar becomes magnetized for a time. Before the
iron bar was magnetized, the molecules within the metal
were lying helter-skelter, their north and south poles
pointing in every which direction.

When you rubbed the piece of iron with a magnet, the
molecules became aligned so that all the north poles were
pointing in one direction within the metal, all the south

poles were pointing the other way.

Intentions work something like that. All the random thoughts, all the dreads and dredging up of unhappy memories, all the unconstructive behaviors and patterns of negative mental and emotional focus become aligned in the direction of the intention. For an intention to work for our well-being, it has to be constructive. When an intention is to work for our highest good, it must be spiritually sound.

The intentions in this book are the fruitage of the illumined consciousness that wears an outer garment named Swami Shankarananda. They were given at different times in different situations, sometimes for a specific need or circumstance of a devotee, sometimes as a general approach to upliftment of mind and heart.

When you work with any positive intention, it is wonderful to offer the intention first thing in the day. Then the message sets the tone for the day. But any of these intentions can be offered any time of day or night with beneficial effects. When offered in the morning, with feeling and conviction, the message of course resounds in the conscious level of mind, and if offered with energy, can sink into the subconscious as well.

You may have heard a church bell chime the hour, and if it is a large bell, the vibration of its sound lingers like an echo after the initial strike. An intention works the same way. After you offer the intention, the echo of it may resound in your awareness and come floating back to you during your day, especially if the mind goes into an area of thought that is contrary to the purity of the intention.

Above all, have fun working with these intentions. Growth in consciousness is not a heavy-duty task, but the best fun of all.

Srimati Shanti Mataji

AUM

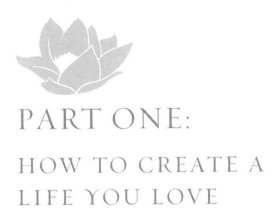

PART ONE:

HOW TO CREATE A LIFE YOU LOVE

What is an intention?

An intention is a well-thought-out and clearly defined expression of the heart's desire. Intentions allow us to gain clarity and precise focus as to what we individually aspire to achieve and realize. An intention incorporates enthusiasm; passionate adherence to one's objective, purpose, or ideal; strong motive; and clear vision. Imagineering—feeling and imagination together—yields magnificent results. This is universal truth and law: What we sow in consciousness and nurture with feeling determines what we harvest in our experience. What we imagine and feel always corresponds to the outcome. Everything in our life is made possible by the law of attraction.

An intention is a vibration, and with intention, you let the universe know how you want to relate to life, to people.

Intentions are:

I nterest in accomplishment

N ature of the desire

T ruth of vision

E manation of feeling

N aturalness of purpose

T rain of thought

I deal of focus

O dyssey of thought

N ecessity of objective

S ecret of motivation

What is the purpose of intentions?

Intentions serve the purpose of giving focus and clarity to the heart's desire and sustaining the focus and clarity with the energy of conviction, the energy of the vision of fulfillment, and the energy of direction to that which is set into motion in the intention.

Lovely intentions are catalysts for realization.

Lovely intentions prepare the way for accomplishment.

Lovely intentions are the harbingers of desire's fulfillment.

Lovely intentions give clear focus to ideals to be fulfilled.

Lovely intentions allow feelings to be known.

Lovely intentions blossom like flowers in the garden of the mind. Pure mind is the abode of pure intentions.

Lovely intentions luminesce the darkness as stars illumine the night.

Lovely intentions energize vision and desire, giving birth to creative expression.

Lovely intentions move along the path of least resistance and attract attention to purposeful imagination.

Lovely intentions express fulfillment of desire in the imagination before they are fulfilled in action.

Lovely intentions allow love to bless the intender.

Why do intentions work?

Intentions invariably bear their results because of the law of magnification or attraction. The whole universe consists of vibrations, and when an intention is focused on with great love and enthusiasm and steadfastness, it causes the corresponding vibratory frequency to pull into your experience the manifestation or materialization of that which is like unto your intention.

In other words, by formulating an intention with feeling and conviction, clarity and pure focus, you magnetize into your experience the support of similar universal vibrations or currents of delivery.

The process of working with intentions undermines the habit of allowing self-doubt or impatience to sabotage your creative endeavor. It also reveals your innate ability to bring into focus and manifestation what contributes to well-being and success. Focusing on an intention corresponds to the scriptural injunction, "Let your eye be single" and your whole consciousness will have the benefit of such one-pointedness. Your focus will illuminate the power and success of your intention.

How do I choose an intention from the many offered in this book?

This is rather simple. It depends on what you are processing or wanting to get more clarity about or cause to be accelerated in your consciousness and experience. Since the intentions are alphabetized, you should have no difficulty in selecting the one that addresses your need. It may be that several seem to meet the requirement.

How do you discern which one to choose of those few, such as two or three? Read them over slowly and reflectively. Speak them aloud because the auditory benefit is that they express your tone of conviction. Pay attention to the energy response from your heart. This will let you know which intention is in alignment with your intention to know what to do or to know

the next step to take in accelerating or deepening the feeling
of the desired outcome.

How many intentions should I work with at a time?

How many meals do you like to eat each day to remain
satisfied? Or how many tasks can you accomplish today?
If you are a novitiate, it is best to concentrate on one
intention until it totally saturates your consciousness or
until you are successful in focusing on it consistently to
eliminate any distractions that may weaken your resolve
to be steadfast in working with an intention. Furthermore,
there must be no doubt in your mind as to the effectiveness
of the intention. Doubt surely arises when we focus on
the objectified result rather than enjoying the creative
process itself.

Once you experience success with this process, you most
assuredly can add another intention, but at a separate time
of the day, until you have success with it. In time, you will
be able to add a number of intentions to your repertoire.
But these must be incorporated slowly so that no confusion
or conflict arises in the mind as to which one is to
be exercised.

Of course, once you see how successful this process of
deliberate intention is, when you focus deliberately on
the creative process of energizing that which you want to

experience, you will always have clarity; and clarity gives the assurance that you are aligned with the corresponding vibration, which carries within it the power of manifestation.

Please note the word "deliberate." This must always be linked with intention. Otherwise your awareness or attention is dispersed. A scattered mind cannot bear the fruit of fulfillment.

What is the best time to offer an intention?

The best times to create or offer an intention are on awakening and before retiring for the night. Ask yourself, "What do I choose to experience?" That will help you establish the intention for that day or during the night.

Of course, it is also good to offer an intention or to create one anytime during the day. If you are working with a particular intention, you can also offer it at different times of the day to reinforce the intention you created or offered on awakening and before going to sleep.

What is the difference between affirmations and intentions?

Affirmations are good for what they are—stepping stones. They are not the goal. Affirmations are wonderful if you're in a state of mental terror, confusion, anxiety, worry, or fear, and you cannot concentrate on peace of mind or joy. At this point, you may not be able to meditate because your mind is in too much turmoil. What you discover when your mind is agitated is that you are repeating something that is making you agitated. Amazing, isn't it? Even when you know exactly what's making you agitated, you keep repeating what is agitating you, and then you wonder why you cannot find peace.

The affirmation serves the function of slowing down the agitated mind and bringing some light into the murky picture that you're holding in your mind. That's good. Now you're feeling a little calmer. You say, "Oh, that feels a little better."

Yet what are you negating in your mind when you use an affirmation? When you affirm something, the implication is that here is something you have to deny, because affirmations have an opposite, do they not? Think about it.

Now you have to be afraid that if you don't declare an affirmation, the thing you do not want will continue in your life. Actually, by pushing against what you do not want in thought and feeling, you are keeping the thing you do not want in your life.

Intentions do not seek to deny or push against what you do not want. They are positive, focused statements and feelings for what you do want.

Is there a distinction between visualization and intentions?

Yes, there's a big difference. Visualization is natural to man. Throughout the day we use our eyes to perceive what's around us. So we are visualizing what's present. The purpose of such visualization is not to produce any specific results.

Then there is focused or intentional visualization, the purpose of which is to energize that which you want to bring into creation. Ordinary visualization is to see what you would like to see. Using imagination goes much further because it includes intention. Why imagine anything unless you intend to benefit from it or experience something you want to experience?

Visualization is limited because it's mental. It doesn't have the energy and the passion behind it to bring what you visualize into expression. When you use your imagination, you are the actor and the participator. So many people fail to realize their dreams because they are mental about it. Reality is not mental. Reality is visceral, kinesthetic, feeling.

Can we transform old beliefs through intentions?

Old beliefs are transformed through new beliefs. In other words, you have to believe you can transform old beliefs through new beliefs. Then you can formulate your intention:

I intend to transform this negative, limiting, or self-defeating belief by replacing it with a more expansive, uplifting, healing and constructive belief.

Then you voice what your constructive belief is. Now you declare: "I believe I have the resources of the universe at my fingertips to manifest whatever is consistent with my belief, my choice."

Are intentions more effective than prayer?

Intentions may or may not be equally effective, even as prayer may not be equally as effective as intentions. To understand, we need to define the meaning of prayer.

What is the purpose of prayer? Is it not your intention or desire through prayer to draw forth a response from the infinite, whether the personal or impersonal aspect of deity? Therefore, you set aside prayer time with the intention to let nothing divert you from your heart's desire to be totally focused on directing all your thoughts to the source of fulfillment. This is intentional prayer.

Now, as to prayerful intention: When you infuse your intention with devotion and the pure desire of the heart, your intention arouses the response of infinite love. One who prays may believe that the response comes from God outside himself or herself. This surely is understandable so long as one believes that there is a separation between the devotee and the deity. When one understands that devotion is the link between devotee and deity, then they are seen to exist within the same field of fertile consciousness and love. When the devotee sees himself at one end of the field and the deity at the other end of the field, this increases in him an intense yearning to get across the field to the source of fulfillment.

Devotional intention, prayerful intention, is intensely effective when one recognizes that the objective is to realize in the present the response or activity of the divine Self, or source. Prayerful intention also rests on the recognition that when I evoke the divine will, that will is always manifested as a loving response to the intentionality of the prayerful individual, or devotee.

Neither intention nor prayer, however, is effective if it lacks focus, clarity of purpose, and innate conviction in the law of universal attraction. Hence, according to one's belief, which incorporates intention and prayer in resonance, will be the corresponding result.

What if someone is adversarial to my intention?

Using intentions is sacred inner work. It is usually best to practice silently around others and not to speak of what you are doing right away. If you take a cake out of the oven too soon, the cake will be ruined. If you speak of your inner work with intentions too soon, meaning before results manifest, there is always the possibility someone will belittle your efforts or point out that your intention doesn't seem to be working. Such comments can create doubts in your mind and weaken your faith in the divine law of manifestation.

On the other hand, suppose someone blasts you with unkind words and says, "I don't like you"—or worse. You are working with an intention to love unconditionally. If you say, "Well, I intend to love you unconditionally," such words may make the other even more adversarial. You can just do your inner work and love the other unconditionally, and the vibration of your love will go forth and reach the other at some level.

In the face of another's judgment or criticism of you, remember—never cater to anyone's limited perspective. See their complaint and verbal attack as a golden opportunity to share the light of expansion that takes them beyond the parameters they have established for themselves to convince themselves there are limitations. Never argue with someone from a limited state of consciousness. Immediately accept the opportunity to expand, to keep expanding beyond someone's claim, difficulty, upset, or restrictive thinking.

> *When seeming differences arise with another, I intend to offer mutual respect, unconditional love, joy, and playfulness.*

> *I choose to connect with the master within who does not interact with another's negativity.*

Another way to defuse the situation is to agree with them. "Be quick to agree with thine adversary." Not that you see them as your adversary necessarily, but they are in a state of adversarial activity. So you agree with them in order to get their attention so that you can introduce a more expansive position. You're meeting them on their terms, but not for the purpose of staying there. Just stay there briefly, because you're on your way to the next bliss experience.

I choose to see each person reconnecting to his or her stream of pure joy, love, clarity, and creativity. It feels wonderful!

What if an intention doesn't work?

Someone said to me, "Swami, my intention didn't turn out for me, no matter what I did." I asked her how it did turn out. When the person told me what happened, I said, "Well, it did turn out. It always turns out." You cannot do something without getting something back. Then she admitted that it didn't turn out the way she expected.

"Ah. It didn't turn out the way you expected? Was your inner work consistent with your expectation? What were you focusing on while you were expecting a good result?"

She said, "I was focusing on the fact that things were not happening as I wanted. I focused on 'what if,' and the doubts came in."

"Well, you overrode your own fulfillment by focusing on what wasn't happening and deserting the fulfillment of your expectations."

You cannot expect something wonderful to happen while you focus on something terrible happening or on what is not happening. What you'll get more of is what is not happening, because there is a divided state of consciousness. That's dualism.

If you expect a wonderful outcome, then you have to focus on the outcome being your reality now, even while you're expecting its externalization in your life. It already exists in the now at the inner level, and it's on the way at the outer level.

I choose to give my loving attention to the feeling that I desire to realize until it is my reality.

We really mess up at times, don't we? Then we blame maya, we blame the world, we blame life, we blame the government, we blame the system, we blame the family, we blame the genes, we blame the DNA coding, we blame some space beings tampering with it, we blame the fact that we cannot sleep, that we have nightmares or horrible memories. The blame game is not the game of life.

To play the game of life well, to succeed, to thrive, meditate on that which expands your awareness. Meditate on that which brings ever greater joy, relief, fulfillment, courage, physical, mental, and emotional well-being, spiritual expansion of consciousness, God-consciousness, consciousness of oneness, bliss-consciousness.

Even though I want to focus on my intention, what if the thought comes that the intention might not work?

If you allow negative thoughts to enter, there will be delays in experiencing your heart's desire. Then you will have to trace back to why things happened the way they did rather than the way you intended. Whatever happens always relates to the law of attraction. This is one of the great guidelines: Life is a Lila, a divine play, and what we sow, we reap. That means what we sow in consciousness, what we project in consciousness, whatever we vibrate, we draw into our experience.

It's not only the words that we say or think. The words have an important role to play, but for the moment, the guideline is to vibrate only the feelings and thoughts we want to keep in circulation. Whatever they are, they are the ones that vibrationally will continue circulating and returning to you a thousandfold.

What a law of magnanimity! You plant one apple seed and you get a tree with thousands upon thousands of apples through the years. Such is the magnanimity of the universe, of the invisible made visible, of the one seed containing the potentiality of thousands of fruits of nurturing, sustaining, life-giving, life-enhancing effects.

I choose to imagine the successful outcome of every one of my intentions.

What happens when you have doubts? You imagine a terrible outcome. You expect good, but you imagine a terrible outcome. What you expect and what you imagine have to be in harmony with each other. If you expect good, but you imagine the worst, or you expect the outcome to be contrary to what you imagine, then what you get is what you expect. What you expect and what you imagine have to be in agreement. When two agree on anything, it is done unto them. When there is disagreement, there is disaster.

Imagination works both ways. If we abuse it or misuse it, it works to our detriment. We have to be careful even when we joke about things. To give you an example about imagining something, there was a little girl who played dress-up. She put on her mother's black dress and the black veil, and the child played the part of the widow. This little girl, day after day, got caught up in the role of wearing widow's weeds. Time passed, she grew into adulthood, and she married a wonderful, loving, caring man who became ill. They hadn't been married for many years when she became a young widow and wore black weeds, just as she had imagined as a little girl.

The thing I imagine with conviction is what I create in my experience. You and I cannot fear anything unless we imagine what we fear. Fear is always about something we don't want to experience, or imagining that we have something that we don't. Fear is about giving power to the world of effects or appearances, rather than remembering that there is only one power operating in the universe that is totally benign, blissful, constructive, and creative. Fear is always about believing that there's something else or something other than divine love operating in the universe.

Remember Job's realization after he had lost everything: "The thing that I feared has come upon me." Likewise, we find out that the thing we dwell on consistently manifests. If someone fears poverty, fears sickness, fears aging, fears loneliness, misunderstandings, or criticism, then they wonder why they experience the effects of their fears. They don't make the connection between the fear of criticism and being criticized, the fear of loss of job and losing the job, the fear of poverty and experiencing poverty.

I choose to remember that I have a choice whether to focus on fear or on love.

What about the words we say or think? You said words have an important role to play.

Indeed, we have to pay attention to the words we send out, because they carry emotion or powerful thought, expectation, or desire. The words we cast upon the water, the vibrations we send out, don't just go out and that's the end of it. The words we cast out upon the water come back to us. So the words we use in our intentions are important,

because the words carry the vibration or feeling behind
their meaning. In fact, all the words we formulate
are important.

If we speak harshly or judgmentally about anybody, the
effect of that will return to the sender, because there is no
separation. Everything we send forth has our signature with
it and the return address, which is our frequency. It will
always find us wherever we are, because it has never left us.
It is extended from us, but it is not separated from us.
This law of return works in our favor when our intentions
are clear and positive and draw on divine consciousness.
When we speak negative words, we obviously would not
be so eager for the return mail.

The intentions offered in this book are spiritually pure,
powerful, God-centered words. That's why they carry
the power to help you create a life you love, when the
intentions are worked with and adhered to and loved
into externalizing what you desire.

How do I use intentions to create my day?

We have infinite power to draw on from within. To
utilize this power to create a wonderful day means that
every day we create intentions, or apply the intentions
we have, for different areas or activities in our life before
we engage in them. Thus, we pre-pave the way to a
wonderful adventure, outcome, and experience.

Here's the way you do that: Before you go to bed, think
about the activities that are ahead of you tomorrow.
As you think about these activities, observe what kind of
message you are sending to yourself about these things
you need to do. Ask yourself if you want that message
delivered to your body at the cellular level. Do you want
to harvest or experience the result of that message?
If not, revise your thoughts and feelings immediately.
Be a revisionist, not a dogmatist.

*My intention is to revise every thought that I have about
tomorrow, relating to any subject, any activity, any
encounter that does not fill me with joy and anticipation.*

Change your thought to one that will fill you with joy and
appreciation. Are you getting that? All you have to do now
is enjoy doing it. It won't take much time if you make it your
intention that it will work immediately.

And if everything in your life falls apart, and there's nothing
left to hold on to, what you're left with is your pure essence
and awareness—and the freedom to create anew, to perceive
your life in a different way than you have, and to allow
for new experiences and adventures based on what you
consciously choose to experience, to realize, to dream
about, to invest your energy in, to invest your love, your
awareness, your appreciation.

*I intend to remember that in the midst of all challenges,
no matter how incomprehensible, the love of the universe*

is supporting my well-being.

*I choose to remember that whatever I'm going through,
no matter how painful, I am on my way Home.*

It's never too late to create happiness, to be a constructive creator of what you want to create in your life.

Will it help to keep a journal of intentions?

I encourage you to keep a journal every day. Keeping such a journal of intentions and your work with them will help you create a life you love. Intentions are our friends. Intentions are born of contrast. Contrast is also your friend, because it lets you know what you want and what's not wanted, or what you want more of and what you want less of.

What is it you intend to experience today that you didn't experience yesterday or that you want to experience more of? Keeping a journal is a good kinesthetic practice. It will be visceral if you write out after your meditation what you intend to bring into your experience today or what you intend to give of yourself to the world today that is a blessing. What belief system do you intend to let go of today or choose to let go of, because the desire of your "I" is on the transformation of those limiting beliefs?

We have been given assistance and guidance to transform

our desires and our perceptions, so that we can live in the
consciousness that "I have no enemies. I have only love to
share." Wouldn't you want to be able to live like that?
Think of making it your intention, and, at the start of
the day, writing it in your journal:

*I intend to share love unconditionally, to radiate it,
to extend it especially to those who are unloving.*

What is the need of those who are unloving? Those who are
mean, selfish, fearful, greedy, and so on? *They need to experience
love!* It's not by condemning anyone that we heal anybody.
It's not by condemning another that we heal our own short-
sightedness, our spiritual myopia. If you want to experience
spiritual utopia, you must renounce spiritual myopia. You
need an eye specialist. In fact, you have to become your own
"I" specialist. Let thine eye be single. Specialize in letting
your eye be single so that you remain single in your
consciousness, that you live and move and have your
being in the consciousness of oneness.

To love others we have to know first, that we are worthy
of God's love and grace, and second, so is the other person.
There is not one valid reason to justify the feeling of
unworthiness, not even one, because God did not create
anything unworthy of Its love, since everything is the creation
of love. How can anything or anyone be unworthy of God's
love? How can God make anyone unworthy of Its own
love? Think on this. You are pure energy, the energy of
God manifesting. You are divine love manifesting.

Keep this intention in your journal and in your mind:

I intend to experience the limitless love of my being.

When you energize an intention, that which is the desire of your intention gains momentum. As it gains momentum, that which you no longer energize loses its momentum. If you want a condition to lose momentum, you have to energize that which you want to have gain momentum in your experience, that which you want to accelerate, to unfold.

Can intentions help me deal with negativity?

The short answer is "yes." Any intent that draws on your inner resources or spiritual consciousness is dynamic and powerful in directing the mind toward the object or goal desired. Intention carries within it expectancy based on the recognition that what you expect or intend to happen is consistent with the energy, feeling, and thought-form, or seed idea, you are eager to set into motion and potentize.

When you launch an intention, the greater your feeling of conviction and joyful anticipation of its fulfillment, the more likely it is for its fulfillment to manifest rather quickly.

There is an important area of consideration that if neglected can cause a delay of the intention bearing fruit or objectifying at all; and that is not allowing the intention to prosper. Once you launch it into the universe, you must make sure that you maintain a positive, disciplined focus as to its outcome rather than entertaining any kind of skepticism or doubt as to its realization.

Doubt is recognized by the expression "What if?" What if it doesn't happen or is not meant to happen, or I am unworthy, or I don't deserve a brilliant outcome. To energize doubt in this manner will replace the former intention with a new one—a negative intention. When you focus on what you don't want to happen, that too is an intention, which can explain non-realization of your original intention.

It is best to develop the consciousness of intentional creation by beginning with a small project that is more likely for your mind to accept, one that will not meet with resistance from your mind or from ego-consciousness.

To make an intention really powerful, you need to be clear why you are offering it in the first place if you doubt it can be realized. What may help you overcome the obstacle of doubt is to understand that when you offer doubt, that doubt is also an intention that it may not work. When you understand the law of cause and effect, then it will be clear to you that what you doubt, you let out vibrationally into the world, even as what you affirm or intend in a positive form will vibrationally go out into the universe. In both cases, the response will not be according to your words but according to the vibrational frequency with which you invest your words or thought-form. Furthermore, impatience is another negative influence in sustaining positive intentions. "Why is it taking so long? What am I doing wrong? Haven't I waited long enough to see results?" Impatience is based on not understanding the law of cause and effect. Impatience can also be a form of intention because you are harboring the thought of impatience. Very curious, is it not? When you focus on impatience, is that not a form of resistance to letting your original intention fulfill itself in its own way and time?

You cannot control how the intention is going to fulfill itself, because that is not within the capacity of the human mind. However, your spontaneous Self—the all-knowing consciousness, the all-powerful creative spirit—alone knows how to orchestrate your intention's fulfillment.

Incidentally, doubt and impatience can also imply that you believe in a withholding God, that is, God is withholding from you the fulfillment of your heart's desire. This is impossible once you realize that the God of the universe and of all manifestations and the fulfillment of the heart's pure desire is unconditional love. Love cannot entertain any such horrible or uncharitable thought or impulse.

What about negative qualities or emotions?

Yes, intentions can help you deal with any negative emotion, such as fear, anger, jealousy, and so on.

Let's look at one form of negativity—judgment. It can be judgment of another or judgment of yourself. In either case, if you want to experience the magnificence of the universe, if you want to live and move and have your being in the glory of God, if you want to participate in the greater works, give yourself a command, an intention:

> *I intend to replace every judgment with an expression of love.*

When you observe a negative quality or emotion within you, please don't be hard on yourself. When you judge yourself, you come from a place of imperfection. When you express love, you come from the understanding that perfection is love, that love is always perfect. Love is never imperfect. Do you realize that love is always perfect, because love is God and love cannot create anything imperfect? Imperfection is always based on judgment. Something may be incomplete, but that doesn't make it imperfect.

> *I intend to replace judgment with understanding. Every time I am tempted to judge, I choose love.*

You also may have to deal with the negativity of the world. Your treasure is where you place your attention. Where is your treasure? The more attention you give to the sorrow of others or the suffering in the world, the more value you are giving to that which upsets you—and the more you are reinforcing the negativity by giving it power.

You always have a choice. You can identify with the horrors of the world, with cruelty, with the feelings you have because you say someone hurt you; or you can simply observe what affects you in a negative way, and whether you want to be affected that way or whether you want to be effective in a positive way. You can use an intention like this to shift your attention to what promotes your well-being and takes you beyond the negativity of those impressions:

> *I deliberately choose to shift my focus from suffering to images, ideas, qualities, and memories that reconnect me with the stream of pure joy, love, light, and thanksgiving.*

Can intentions help me realize God?

Intentions can help you realize or fulfill any desire, including the desire for God-realization. One who yearns to realize God is a disciple of truth, the truth of their being.

A devotee, or disciple of truth, is deliberate and conscientious about offering clear and powerful intentions to accomplish his tasks and realize his divine aspirations. Intention goes far beyond wishful thinking, for it is energized by the power of will, clarity of vision, and unity of purpose to realize the heart's desire. Divine will power is the source of intention and the gift of your inner being. Your life will improve day by day as you create intentions that promote well-being, harmony, peace, loving relationships, and the well-being of all. This is an integral quality of the devotee who yearns for Self-realization.

I choose to be happy, joyful, blissful, and to allow everyone else to be who they are because I value the reality of peace, joy, harmony, and oneness.

What are the inner guidelines for working with intentions and manifesting my heart's desire?

These steps can be guidelines for consciously creating your experiences; they can be used in creating and offering intentions, and in realizing your divinity. The secret of successfully manifesting any aspect of your creativity, of being filled with the passion to manifest your divinity in experience in this physical reality, starts with these steps:

1. **Be clear about your heart's desire.**
   We have to know what we want to experience or realize or manifest. Then we have to reflect on whether the image is so clear that it goes beyond being a vague thought or a vague desire.

2. **Move into the feeling of fulfillment.**
   Once I have a clear image of the ideal or the objective, on whatever level of manifestation it may be, I have to go from the desire—if it is to blossom and bear fruit— to the place of fulfillment within consciousness.

3. Bring the feeling fully into the heart.

Then I have to bring the feeling into the heart to water it with devotion, which means to pour the nectar of divine love into the feeling of fulfillment, to drench that feeling in love.

4. Assume the feeling of joyful birthing.

I have to bring the feeling into the heart until I feel impregnated with the reality of that, so that I really feel that which I have Self-conceived is ready to be born, that it's bulging, pressing heavily against the walls of physical reality. We have to be our own midwife to deliver it by acting in consciousness from the assumed feeling of joyful birthing.

5. Express gratitude for the fulfillment of your heart's desire.

Express your joy and appreciation for that to which you have given birth, and offer gratitude that it is coming now into your experience as an extension of yourself.

6. Move into the conversation of success.

This next step in having a successful delivery is the one that is most commonly missed, because most people hold onto the desire for a successful delivery rather than focusing on the successful delivery. The way to move past the desire for the successful delivery is to move into the conversation you'd be having after you have had a successful delivery. You'd be no longer speaking of your desire; you'd be speaking from the standpoint of the successful delivery.

7. Trust God's grace.
Trust has to do with remaining loyal to your heartfelt
desire. It's as simple as that, as graphic as that, as visceral
as that. People may say your heart's desire is impossible
because of the outer picture. Impossible has to do only
with what people are focusing on, rather than on what is.
People convince themselves that something is impossible
only because they don't know how to make it possible.
Therefore, they decide it is impossible. You lock yourself
into claiming that it's impossible because everyone else has
decreed it's impossible. Belief systems, institutions, limited
perspective, lack of vision all contribute to that claim.
Love has never heard of something being impossible.

This is how we successfully create, give birth, or deliver the
goods. You can get pregnant again right away. With this inner
process of manifestation, you don't have to wait. It's not like
human birth where you have to heal first or get plenty of rest.

Practice the activity of these seven steps with every desire,
every intention you put forth, every yearning to manifest
some quality or experience, including the longing for
God-realization.

Can I create my own intentions? If so, what would be the guidelines for creating them?

This is a very good question, a very important one. Everyone
is capable of creating his or her own intentions. In fact, most

of the time you do it unwittingly, without realizing that everything you experience is the expression of an intention you put out into the universe, whether the thought is negative or positive, whether a desire is uplifting or degrading, whether the vision is expansive or restrictive, whether the feeling is loving or unloving. These are all components of creating intentions, consciously or unconsciously. Understanding this, we can now begin by making it our intention:

I intend at all times to focus only on what is desirable, loving, constructive, liberating, healing, peace-generating, and conducive to joyful adventures and positive relationships.

Translating that into practical self-application means that I understand I am the creator of my experiences. Very often, when confusion and lack of clarity prevail, and worry or fear inter*fear* (interfere) with uplifting one's consciousness or shifting from focusing on what is hurtful, frightening, or depressing, conscious intentions become a springboard for moving forward out of any negative state of mind. This requires clarity, focus, and passion in accessing the thought, feeling, and image that would fill the canvas of the mind with a desirable outcome.

For example, after seeing the doctor and receiving a negative report based on X-rays or other medically predetermined statistics regarding your condition, it is easy to get caught up in fear. Ask yourself: What do you see when you are trapped in fear regarding your situation and projected outcome? Not a pretty picture, is it? Not something you would like to see happen. And yet, it does happen because you are putting out a negative intention such as, "I will die of this illness, or at least, it will get worse. I will be left helpless. People will not love me anymore, because no one likes to be around a sick person. I don't know where to turn for help."

It takes very little time to recall such an experience in your life. It also takes little reflection to recall how you judged yourself or heard others judge you, claiming that obviously it is your karma or God is punishing you or you have done something wrong, sinful, or evil. Or you have inherited this illness from your family. None of these judgments and condemnations help you feel better, heal, or hope for a better tomorrow. Such is the impact of collective consciousness or personal judgment. Fortunately, you no longer need to be the victim of helplessness, powerlessness, and seemingly external powers and negative influences.

Now we come to the power of intentions in putting you on a different track, the track of well-being, freedom, self-empowerment, self-remembrance. It is vitally important for everyone who wants to create intentions to remember the supreme purpose is to help one come to self-remembrance as to who one is, for only then can one realize the power of being master of one's life and creating any kind of life one chooses, prefers, or intends to live. It requires utmost self-scrutiny and spiritual discernment to dislodge all self-flagellating attitudes, mortifying thoughts, negative beliefs and attitudes. Once you intend to be the observer of these factors or conditions within your mind, you do not as an observer attach yourself to your observations. This means you detach from the petty I-consciousness, or ego-centeredness, by no longer identifying yourself as these conditions or circumstances. Instead, you make this your intention:

I intend to be the impartial observer of whatever state of consciousness I am experiencing.

Then you simply can intend to let it pass, and it will. There is an important reason that it must. Only so long as you energize any image, condition, memory, untruth, relative fact or statistic, or outside influences, can they persist in your experience and give birth to similar conditions. The key is not to dwell on what you observe when your observation keeps you in a state of negativity or self-limitation, unworthiness, self-recrimination, or helplessness. You have the power to create the most powerful and magnificent intentions in the midst of your observations by identifying what you would prefer to experience, to see, to hear, and to relate to. Once you have decided what you prefer, you are now in a position to assert your divine ability to create any number of intentions that move you out of your present state of hurtfulness, anxiety, worry, insecurity, sense of lack, unworthiness, powerlessness, unlovingness, lack of joy, and so on.

In your intention, you incorporate or express only positive scenarios that, by the law of attraction, will marshal and galvanize the benign forces and intelligences of the universe (enlightened beings) to assist you in bringing into manifestation your noble and loving intentions. It is not your job or responsibility to figure out how the universe (all that is the expression of the divine source) will bring it about. Leave the details to God, or your creative omniscient Self. Rest in the feeling of fulfillment contrary to physical evidence, and you will succeed step by step. Indeed, you will succeed magnificently in transforming your life from a state of helplessness and fear, worthlessness and inadequacy, into one who can claim that the will, or the divine intention of the creative source, is responding always to my alignment with it.

I am always aligned with the divine will when I am feeling, expressing, sharing, and resonating with unconditional love and purity of consciousness within myself and within everyone.

You will always know whether an intention is "right" for you, or righteous, by the resonance that is created within you between feeling, desire, image, and belief. That is, when these are in agreement in your aspiration for greater well-being, success, expression of love, freedom, and blissfulness, then you are on the right track, the track of ever greater joyous experiences in this intentional universe of manifestation.

One admonishment: When you offer an intention in all purity of heart, with clarity and pure focus, you cannot benefit if you judge or expect it to be ineffective because you are looking for immediate results on the physical plane. To wipe out that delusion or false sense of direction, you need to remember the law of universal attraction: That which you focus on is drawn to you. If your focus lacks persistence or sustenance of love and trust, you are sabotaging your own well-being or success. Assert the divinity of your soul in the face of all opposition and prolonged appearances by nurturing a thankful heart for the consistency of the law of attraction in manifestation. Simply intend to remember: Subjective creation with intention precedes physical manifestation, not according to your time schedule, but according to the law of wisdom that is the jurisdiction of your soul and will never fail to guide you to the best outcome imaginable.

So be it.

Would you summarize how to work with intentions?

First, choose or create an intention:
I intend to feel better. I intend to feel stronger…
or whatever you want to address.

Then you acknowledge:
I acknowledge that it is my nature to be well
(well applying to whatever area of life in which you
want to feel better).

Then you focus:
I choose to give my undivided attention to that which
I choose to experience, be, or realize.

Intention, acknowledgment, and focus—when you bring all three into your conscious awareness, then you will experience that which you initially had to pretend, because it's something you wanted to experience. Then you elicit from your subconscious, your inner consciousness, the responsiveness of that vibration, that energy.

I choose to focus on the polestar of my life, the most blessed thought, ideal, and desire that keeps me on course.

I acknowledge with gratitude that every intention sustained with love and self-allowance becomes reality.

I intend to be transformed by the application of every one of these intentions. I give thanks in advance for their fulfillment in the resurrection of my spiritual identity and unconditional love.

May these words bear much fruit in your experience.
May they bring solace, strength, and nourishment.

May they be a lamp under your feet and a light unto your path.

Swami Shankarananda

AUM SHANTI SHANTI SHANTI

PART TWO:
1001 INTENTIONS

ABUNDANCE

ༀ I choose to share what I have, knowing that more will come.

ༀ I choose to use every thought to promote abundant well-being.

ༀ I intend to live a life of lavish abundance, joyous adventures, and rewarding, creative, self-expression. It feels wonderful!

ༀ I choose to be totally in love with what I'm doing, the secret of success.

ༀ I choose to vibrate with the kind of livelihood that is consistent with my highest good and allows me to experience a lavish income, with mutual benefit to all.

ༀ I choose to replace the idea of spending with investing all thought, energy, time, appreciation, and effort to promote abundant well-being and love.

ༀ I choose to be willing to receive.

ༀ I choose to remember all that the Father has, I have.

ༀ I intend to see abundance manifesting everywhere.

ༀ I intend to flourish in whatever I do that supports mutual well-being, success, and prosperity.

ༀ I choose to bless signs of abundance wherever I see them, knowing all I bless is magnified in my own life.

ༀ I choose to give thanks for my livelihood now while unfolding my livelihood to come.

ༀ I choose to experience a livelihood of ease and grace.

ༀ I intend at all times to recognize the grace of the Beloved operating through others.

ༀ I choose to live by the grace of God, knowing I will always have enough.

ༀ I intend to be more consciously and deliberately connected with the law of abundance and God's presence within me to celebrate life instead of condemning it.

ༀ I choose to embrace God as the law of prosperity and allow that prosperity to come into my experience.

ༀ I choose to be available 24 hours a day to the very best the universe has to offer.

ॐ I choose to acknowledge that I can only receive that which I allow into my consciousness without resistance.

ॐ I choose to give thanks to the Father for dissolving my daily debts as I see them dissolved and to pay off my debts in the present, consistent with my income.

ॐ By the grace of the Beloved, I choose to be the recipient of the abundance of the universe in exchange for the abundant and joyful sharing of energy.

ॐ I choose financial freedom, which allows me to manifest whatever I desire by the grace of Self-love.

ॐ I choose to remember that as I create my heart's desire in my imagination, it is affordable and doable.

ॐ I intend to self-correct every sense of lack by choosing the feeling of abundance—abundant joy, freedom, appreciation, and well-being.

ॐ I choose to be alive to all that is available.

ॐ I intend to honor God's blessings unto me by letting them multiply in my experience and by sharing them unceasingly.

ॐ I intend to flourish in all I do because my God is a flourishing God.

ॐ I choose to put God first, knowing the God that I Am provides me with all the resources I could ever need.

ॐ I intend to ask with the understanding that I will receive and with the intention of allowing it to happen.

ॐ I choose to use everything I see as lack to catapult me into the consciousness of abundance.

ॐ I choose to acknowledge that the more I give, the more I have, for both giving and receiving are infinite.

ॐ I choose to realize that I can never, never, never exhaust the abundance that is God.

ALLOWANCE

꙰ I choose to accept everyone the way an infant accepts one and all with the joy of its being—spontaneously, nonjudgmentally, and eagerly.

꙰ I intend to allow all beings to experience whatever they experience because it's their journey.

꙰ I choose to be happy and allow all persons to be who they are without attempting to change them.

꙰ I choose to support the heart's desire of everyone even if it is not my own.

꙰ I intend to allow everyone to love to his or her capacity.

꙰ I choose to allow another to be indifferent, for I choose Self-love.

꙰ I choose to acknowledge that everyone is exercising their freedom of choice to create and attract all of their experiences and environments, for that allows them to gain greater self-mastery and realization.

꙰ I choose to love unconditionally and to accept and allow everything to be what it is.

ॐ I intend to allow everyone total freedom of choice without judgment, knowing that there are only choices and experiences.

ॐ I choose to be happy, joyful, blissful and to allow everyone else to be who they are because I value the reality of peace, joy, harmony, and oneness.

BEING PRESENT

ॐ I choose to live in the joy of the present moment.

ॐ I choose to feel the sacredness of life from moment to moment.

ॐ I intend to give loving attention to whatever presents itself to me at all times.

ॐ I acknowledge that all transformation takes place in the present. Therefore, I lovingly choose to practice being present, being lovingly mindful. It feels wonderful!

ॐ I intend to see that everyone brings a present to me— the presence of God.

ॐ I choose to be thankful for the presence of God at all times.

ॐ I choose to breathe into the heart to connect with the Beloved. Thank you, Beloved, for being here for me.

ॐ I intend to move into total attentive acceptance of present awareness.

ॐ I choose to allow the presence of God to overwhelm me, now.

ॐ I choose to remember that wherever I am is holy ground. Wherever I am, I am enveloped by the love of God.

ॐ I choose to dwell in the ever present, unconditional love of my heart and the perfection of my being.

ॐ I intend to stay fully present to each moment, that it may unfold fully in its grace, beauty, and purity.

ॐ I intend to bring my mind back to the moment whenever it strays.

ॐ I choose to abide in the remembrance that every moment is God's grace.

ॐ I choose to celebrate the breath of God with every breath I take, for God is the breath of life I receive and God is the breath of life I share.

ॐ On the inhalation, I choose to receive the goodness of God. On the exhalation, I choose to carry this blessing to the world.

ॐ I choose to acknowledge that no moment is more powerful than this moment, for it is God's grace.

ॐ I intend to pay attention to wakefulness.

ॐ I intend to practice loving mindfulness at all times.

ॐ I choose to be in the present, where everything is.

ॐ I choose the simplicity of being by abiding in the heart of love.

BODY TEMPLE

ॐ I choose to see my body as the living temple of God.

ॐ I intend to renew the cells in my body by flooding them with divine love.

ॐ I intend to honor and respect my body, but I am not my body. I am one and identified with the Creator of this body.

ॐ I choose to love my body and to focus on all that is well about it.

ॐ I choose self-love and physical fitness.

ॐ I choose to enjoy everything with the senses by remembering everything I enjoy is the gift of God— God enjoying His gifts.

ॐ I choose to find out what will help me reduce stress.

ॐ I choose to remember how blessed I am that the Beloved has chosen to make this body His temple.

ॐ I choose to acknowledge that everything I eat is the grace of God. Divine wisdom within me perfectly digests, assimilates, and transforms physical substance into physical strength, harmony, and well-being.

ॐ I choose to welcome and allow the divine intelligence within me to maintain my body-temple in perfect health and physical fitness.

ॐ I choose to sanctify all of my senses, recognizing they are sacred vessels for the outpouring of Holy Spirit (the spirit of wholeness, the grace of spirit, of joy, of truth, creative ideas, longevity, enthusiasm, passion, freedom, creative ideas, and playfulness).

ॐ It is my intention to experience God using every particle of my body to manifest through me as energy, life force, movement, strength, rejuvenation, calmness, vibrant health, radiant well-being, and joy of expressing in and through this temple of mine.

COURAGE AND STRENGTH

ॐ I intend to be spiritually strong, like the sunlight that does not stop shining.

ॐ I choose to connect with the courage and strength within me that overcomes every weakness.

ॐ I choose the courage to present myself before the Beloved in the nakedness of my being, knowing nothing is hidden, and I am totally loved and supported in my transformation.

ॐ I choose to go forth bearing the shield of light to deflect anything that is not the light.

ॐ I fearlessly allow the purity and power of truth to expose every form of resistance embedded in my conscious or subconscious state of mind, without resistance.

ॐ In the midst of weakness, I choose to align myself with the remembrance that God is my strength and support. Resting in this inner assurance, I experience the power of fearlessness.

ॐ I choose the courage to risk everything to realize who I Am.

ॐ I intend to remember that in the midst of all challenges, no matter how incomprehensible, the love of the universe is supporting my well-being.

ॐ I choose the courage to embrace all my weaknesses as an offering to the Beloved.

ॐ I choose to abide in unconditional love, which dissolves all fears and connects me with the courage within.

ॐ I choose to be present to the Lord, who is my strength.

CREATIVITY AND IMAGINATION*

ॐ I choose to celebrate the fruitfulness of my creative imagination, which is God.

ॐ I choose to create as many intentions as necessary to move me from where I am to where I choose to be within my heart. As my intention goes, so my life grows.

ॐ I choose to be a powerful attractor for everything that makes my heart sing, my spirit soar, and my resources flourish.

ॐ It is my intention to realize fully that the Father within me is the source of everything I could desire.

ॐ O Universe of my Soul, I choose to give you power of attorney to take charge of my heart's desires.

ॐ I choose to invite the universe to orchestrate the fulfillment of every desire.

ॐ It is my passionate and deliberate intention to ask and allow myself to receive the fulfillment of my heart's desire with feeling and imagination.

ॐ I choose to enter into the joyous adventure of feeling the fulfillment of my heart's desire.

ॐ I intend to manifest only that which is consistent with my expanded Self.

ॐ I intend to desire and realize all that God desires.

ॐ I intend to give pure thought to whatever I imagine to be for my highest good.

ॐ I choose to have fun imagining all that I choose to experience.

ॐ I choose to accept my heart's desire as God's gift to me.

ॐ I intend to imagine that I am now where I'd love to be—physically, emotionally, mentally, and spiritually.

ॐ I choose to imagine the successful outcome of every one of my intentions.

ॐ I choose what I want to bring into my life, and then I choose to fall in love with it.

ॐ I choose to align myself with the nature of love's activity, which is responsiveness.

ॐ I choose for my creative imagination to manifest that which I desire to create for the joy of it.

ॐ I intend to observe how the universe responds to my creative consciousness.

ॐ I choose to do the best I can from moment to moment, for this is fulfillment.

ॐ I choose to give thanks for creativity and to bless the feeling of fulfillment that would be mine as it manifests.

ॐ I choose to build the consciousness of being, doing, and loving that which I want to be, do, and love.

ॐ By the grace of the Beloved, I choose to remember my heart's desires are always fulfilled on time.

ॐ I choose to trust the infinite and remember how it has blessed me in the past. (Trust is the key to reconnect with the fruits of creativity.)

ॐ I choose to stay consciously connected to the ever present source of all manifestations.

ॐ I choose to give my loving attention to the feeling that I desire to realize until it is my reality.

ॐ I intend to enter into the feeling of having and being that which is my heart's desire.

ॐ I choose to focus on the inner reality of my heart's desire, merging with the feeling in total conviction.

ॐ I intend with great joy and love to cultivate whatever talent I have, that it may bless my life and the life of everyone.

ॐ I choose to love my talents with all my heart and Soul.

ॐ I choose to create out of fullness—the only way to create.

*When we acknowledge as the ancient sages taught, that the whole universe and everything within it is the creative expression of the Image-maker, God, it must follow that the Image-maker is the imagination; and whatever we, as expressions of the divine imagination, envision and focus on with love, with deep respect and appreciation will perpetuate itself in our experience.

Therefore, let us not belittle the imagination, the image-maker power, for without it, nothing can come into being. Whatever image we hold in mind and love with our heart will have behind it the energy to manifest as effect in our world. We therefore must be careful what we imagine, or image, especially with intensity of feeling or emotion; for what is or is not wanted, loved or resisted, must manifest in our experience. It is law.

DISCERNMENT

ॐ I choose my words wisely so that I will never want to take them back.

ॐ I intend to witness conditioning (a pattern) as it arises without entering into it.

ॐ I choose to be aware of my predominant thought about my life throughout the day.

ॐ I choose to extract wisdom and value from all my experiences.

ॐ I choose to be willing to look beyond appearances consistently.

ॐ I intend to die to old ideas so that new and better ideas may enrich my mind.

ॐ I choose to allow the light to operate so that limiting patterns cannot thwart my freedom to dwell in joy.

ॐ The moment I observe discomfort, I choose to do that which makes me happier.

ॐ I intend to allow my discernment to contribute to my well-being from moment to moment.

ॐ I intend to use everything I learn to show me the next step.

ॐ I choose to surrender the tyranny of my mind to the consciousness of God within me.

ॐ I choose to turn to that which is unconditioned in the midst of the conditioning.

ॐ I intend to discern the voice of the Beloved in all voices and to see the unfoldment of divine purpose through all experiences.

ॐ I intend to decide the state of consciousness in which I want to leave this world and then to do everything I can from moment to moment to be ready for that state of consciousness.

ॐ I choose to make wisdom and love my guide in life.

ॐ I choose to use spiritual discernment to drive out everything that keeps me from experiencing love.

ॐ I choose to remember I am the father of every thought I have, and I choose to spawn only thoughts I love.

ॐ I choose to observe a situation only long enough to decide on a focus that makes me feel better. (Judgment is dwelling long enough on a situation to feel worse.)

ॐ I choose to identify what I've been thinking by how I feel. I choose to focus only on what feels wonderful.

ॐ I choose to increase my attention to what I want to experience and decrease my attention to what I no longer choose to experience.

ॐ I intend to choose my thoughts mindfully, instead of allowing them to choose me.

ॐ I choose to surrender to the wisdom of each experience with a grateful heart.

ॐ Upon awakening, I intend to choose what I want to create with my thoughts this day.

ॐ It is my intention to discover better ways to do what I have been doing.

ॐ In all I do, I choose to realize that I have come to play a role and to remember a role is not who I Am.

ॐ I intend to be spiritually discerning regarding every aspect of my life by focusing on what contributes to my feeling of well-being and what does not.

ॐ I choose to examine every concept and to ask: Does this concept support Self-love?

ॐ I choose to use the lance of spiritual discernment to lance all illusion.

ॐ I choose with total clarity to reflect before acting on any issue or claim presented to my senses.

ॐ I intend to rejoice in the understanding that, in spite of my conditioning (patterns), there is something within me that persists in seeking to go beyond conditioning.

ॐ I choose to see the value of experiences that seem like darkness.

ॐ I choose to remember that spiritual discernment is to be alive to that which is.

ॐ I choose to focus on the source of all effects, for I cannot be aware of something that is outside of my consciousness.

ॐ I choose to learn from every experience what I have not learned before.

ॐ I intend to build with my mind a love of life and a life of love.

ॐ I intend to learn from my mistake so I won't repeat it.

ॐ I make it my intention and mission throughout the day to choose to hear only the good news (that which is healing, uplifting, and joyful, that which provides positive understanding, input and output).

ॐ I choose to observe when suffering is present and to acknowledge the one observing suffering is not experiencing it.

ॐ I choose to see the value of each experience to my total growth.

ॐ I intend to rise above the pairs of opposites by focusing on that which is beyond the pairs of opposites.*

ॐ I choose to see beyond the sense of limitation to what I want to experience.

ॐ I choose always to let my feeling reveal to me the thoughts that attracted the feeling. (In this way, I determine that loving thoughts create loving feelings, even as unloving thoughts create unloving feelings.)

ॐ I choose to wait until I am guided to spiritual action, instead of reacting and allowing my ego to be in charge.

ॐ I intend at all times to be consciously aware of what I accept in my consciousness and what I do not accept.

*Such as pleasure and pain, good and bad, loss and gain, victory and defeat.

EXPANDED UNDERSTANDING

๑ I choose to understand everything with an open heart.

๑ I choose to understand with my whole being and
knowingness of my heart.

๑ I choose to be eager to understand. I am so excited
about the understanding that is coming to me!

๑ I choose to soothe another's anger by understanding it.

๑ I choose to recognize the greater understanding I
have gained that will help me move beyond this
present experience.

๑ I choose to seek greater understanding than I
realize now.

๑ I choose to go beyond the appearance to really
understand another.

๑ I choose to go to the Father within and have the Father
direct me as to what I need to perceive and understand.

๑ I choose to ask God to grant me the harmony between
mind and feeling, between the intellect and the heart,
for greater understanding.

ॐ I choose to be receptive to what else there is for me to know and to understand.

ॐ I choose to bless my present experience and the understanding it brings.

ॐ I intend to see everything as a message from You, O God.

FAITH

꣓ I choose to cultivate faith, for when my faith is strong enough, anything is possible.

꣓ I choose to express more faith today than I did yesterday.

꣓ I choose to enter into complete faith in my heart's desire.

꣓ I choose to connect with my faith, a powerful antidepressant.

꣓ I choose to allow myself to feel the power of believing that my present experience is to the good of my Self-unfoldment.

꣓ I intend to give my attention to what I choose to manifest, for this is faith, the substance of all that appears.

꣓ I choose to be willing to accept the faith God has in me.

꣓ I choose to put my feeling nature totally into that which I want to bring forth, for faith is feeling.

꣓ I choose to have total faith in the Invisible as the source of the visible.

꣓ I choose to have faith in the power of love that lifts me out of any state of limitation.

FORGIVENESS

ॐ I choose to forgive everyone I hold responsible
for anything.

ॐ I choose not to withdraw love from even the greatest
transgressor.

ॐ I choose to let go of unforgivingness.

ॐ I choose to bless my enemies by entering into a state of
Bliss-consciousness, by radiating love through the
connection with the love in all.

ॐ I choose to judge no one, whether they love or do not love.

ॐ I choose to forgive myself for having forgotten for a
moment that I am divine and so are all.

ॐ For peace in my heart, I choose to forgive everyone who
has ever wronged me, whom I have allowed to hurt me.

ॐ I choose to forgive myself for having held on to painful
images, for focusing on what doesn't feel good.

ॐ I choose to forgive others for being a catalyst for me
to react.*

ॐ I choose to feel better whether another forgives me or not.

ॐ I choose the practice of forgiveness, for it feeds my heart with love.

ॐ I choose unconditional love, which never judges and has nothing and no one to forgive.

ॐ I choose forgiveness, which is a divine quality and always available.

ॐ I choose to rejoice in my ability to experience self-forgiveness.

ॐ I choose to constantly replace disharmonious thoughts and feelings with harmonious ones, for this is forgiveness.

ॐ I choose to forgive everyone I have ever held in bondage, including myself.

ॐ I choose to forgive myself for everything from moment to moment.

ॐ I choose to practice forgiveness 24/7, giving myself to that which is healing.

ॐ I choose to replace every uncharitable thought with the grace of love.

ॐ When others say or do something hurtful, I choose to accept them as they are, for they know not what they do or say.

ॐ I choose to bless the one who has enmity toward me, for he or she is unhappy.

ॐ I choose to be divinely selfish by loving my enemies.

*Reaction is negative, whereas response is positive.

FREEDOM

❀ I intend to be free to create a life for myself that makes my heart sing.

❀ I choose to embrace the freedom to be happy in any situation.

❀ I intend to find joy by exercising freedom of choice without needing anyone's permission but my own.

❀ I intend to change every agreement I have made when it no longer supports my freedom of choice.

❀ I choose to realize that I am a free being living in the consciousness of liberation now.

❀ I choose to accept my freedom to grow in joy, love, wisdom, and understanding.

❀ I choose to realize that the consciousness I Am is limitless, for this is freedom.

❀ I choose the freedom in each moment to make a better choice.

❀ I choose to combine feeling with belief to achieve freedom.

ॐ In the midst of fear, I acknowledge the freedom to choose love.

ॐ I choose from this day forward to exercise the power of freedom within me to experience whatever I want.

GRATITUDE

ॐ I choose to go on a rampage of gratitude for everything in my life.

ॐ I intend to acknowledge with gratitude that everything comes from the Source through my brothers and sisters.

ॐ I intend to focus only on that which makes my heart sing with gratitude.

ॐ I choose to give thanks to be in a position to share and receive so much light.

ॐ I choose to appreciate my awareness of what's going on.

ॐ I choose to give thanks to the universe of my being, for all that I am receiving and experiencing by the powerful, deliberate creating of my imagination and heartfelt gratitude.

ॐ I intend to cultivate the consciousness of gratitude that takes me beyond giving power to the appearances and shatters the illusion of lack and helplessness.

ॐ I intend to bless everything I have with every breath I take and to bless everything that others have with every breath I take.

ॐ I choose to express gratitude for the steps I've taken and for being shown the next step.

ॐ I intend to remember at all times that the Universe is my supply and well-being. I rejoice and give thanks.

ॐ I choose to enter into the gates of thanksgiving and the inner courts of praise.

ॐ I choose to allow my heart to melt in gratitude as I gain ever greater realization that the Beloved's love is beyond all judgment.

ॐ I choose to shift from the feeling of regret to appreciation for what I have learned from my experience.

ॐ I choose gratitude, the shortest bridge to well-being.

ॐ I choose to focus on all that I appreciate in life, instead of what I do not appreciate.

ॐ I choose to give thanks for every experience of contrast, because it makes me eager to transcend all limitations that contrast indicates.

ॐ I choose to find something that I appreciate from moment to moment.

ॐ I intend to appreciate the best that is within me and in everyone else.

ॐ I choose to give thanks for my temporary setbacks, because they remind me of what I love to do, to share, and to receive through love.

ॐ I choose to give thanks for the opportunity in all situations to shower the power of love that I Am.

ॐ When I feel any form of lack, I immediately choose to focus on what I do have and to feel tremendously grateful.

ॐ I choose to be thankful for the conditions that give opportunity for new understanding and desire for greater well-being and new intentions.

ॐ I rejoice and give thanks unceasingly for this embodiment and for every blessing that I allow to flow into my stream of being.

ॐ I choose to live in thankfulness, the quickest way to renounce bitterness of heart, anxiety, and complaints.

ॐ I intend to find countless reasons to be thankful.

ॐ By the grace of the Beloved, I choose to live by the grace of infinite gratitude. I Am, I Am, I Am the grace of the Beloved.

ॐ I choose to give thanks for my desire to improve my life and what I have.

ॐ I choose to give thanks for the divine plan of my life that is unfolding day by day.

ॐ I choose to give thanks for my peace and abundance now.

HEALING

ॐ I choose to abide in love, which alone can heal.

ॐ My clear, passionate, powerful intention is to be a pure conduit of healing, unconditional love from moment to moment and to radiate love to all beings throughout the universe.

ॐ I intend always to enjoy excellent health because God is my health.

ॐ I choose to allow the unconditional love that I Am eagerly to meet anyone who is calling for help and healing.

ॐ I choose to joyfully radiate healing love to everyone everywhere.

ॐ I intend to turn my light to everything that can be transformed by the light.

ॐ I intend to bless everyone who comes into my awareness by beholding God working through everyone and in every situation.

ॐ I choose to appreciate wholeness, which is always available.

ॐ I intend to see every murky stream of consciousness that has been flowing through me being transformed by the stream of pure intention into the light.

ॐ I intend at all times to be totally immersed in the healing consciousness with everyone and with all situations.

ॐ By the grace of the Beloved, I am inspired and blessed to see and to nurture the wholeness of being in everyone.

ॐ I intend to feel the power of healing love within me that is in charge of all my unconscious activities.

ॐ I choose to speak only words that are healing.

ॐ I choose to remember that the Source is the only power in the universe that can heal, uplift, and inspire us.

ॐ I choose to give thanks to the Father for my perfect health now.

ॐ I choose to exercise a powerful healing influence on all those who are suffering.

ॐ When a person comes to mind who is experiencing difficulty, I choose to see the word "love" over his or her head like a banner, blazing with golden light, expanding and spreading.

ॐ I choose to focus only on another's health, healing, and miraculous recovery on all levels.

꙼ I choose to focus on wholeness, for whatever I focus on in another is magnified in the other's experience as well as in my own.

꙼ Whenever I am aware of suffering, I choose to place my consciousness on love.

꙼ I choose to ask the Beloved to use me in whatever way will be healing to the world.

꙼ I intend to bear witness to the glory of God rather than the sufferings of humanity.

꙼ I choose to allow my inner monitor to constantly guide me to release quickly any unhealthy impressions and toxicity that come to me throughout the day.

꙼ I choose to see a stream of liquid light flowing, carrying any dark spot out of another's energy field or my own.

꙼ I intend to choose from moment to moment what is healing, uplifting, and joy-fulfilling.

꙼ I choose to focus on health as my natural state until it feels familiar and natural again.

꙼ I choose to align with the one healing presence, the only power, reestablishing harmony and wholeness within the body, mind, and spirit.

ॐ I choose to be willing to change any habits that cause illness.

ॐ I choose to acknowledge another's pain and his or her ability to overcome the pain all the more.

ॐ When I am aware of pain, I choose to give my total focus to healing.

ॐ I intend to see all wounds healed the moment they come to my attention.

ॐ I intend to welcome the stream of pure healing love, that it may flow freely through me to everyone and everything around me.

ॐ I choose to imagine glorious light pouring through the top of my head, through my crown chakra, filling my heart. I feel it move through every cell, blessing me, blessing the world.

ॐ I choose to offer joy in place of sadness, sanity in place of madness, health in place of illness, and wealth in place of poverty, remembering that success is always available.

ॐ I choose to see a beam of light going to [name of person or area], filling [him, her, them, or it] with revitalizing, healing light and love, permeating every particle of space with uplifting and illuminating vibrations.

ॐ I choose to give up the idea of sickness and focus on total connection with the Source, fulfilling the conditions of being whole.

ॐ I choose to see everyone growing rather than suffering.

ॐ I choose to shift my attention from what I want to heal to what I want to experience.

ॐ I choose to look past appearances consistently to be with wholeness—my own and others.

ॐ I choose to remember that which I Am is saturating the Earth with healing love.

ॐ I choose to have the willingness to be made whole.

ॐ It is my intention to be available to those who have suffered as I have suffered.

ॐ I choose to focus on how another was before they needed help.

ॐ I choose to allow the healing power to be active within me and to flow out through me to all who reach out for love.

ॐ I choose to keep growing, remembering that this is how healing takes place.

ॐ I choose to ask God to speak Its words through me, words that will help another.

ॐ I choose to fast from every negative perception, belief, and attitude in order to experience wholeness.

ॐ I choose to see each person reconnecting to his or her stream of pure joy, love, clarity, and creativity. It feels wonderful!

ॐ I choose to vibrate to [name of person] waves of luminous love and electrifying joy in realization of our oneness and the radiance of [his or her] soul.

ॐ I choose to see anyone who comes to mind as a recipient of the light, until there is only light.

ॐ I choose to look more deeply into the well to discover my wellness, my wholeness, and the wholeness of everyone.

ॐ My intention is to release from every cell in my body and on every level of my being every limitation that I have ever experienced by welcoming and accepting this light of healing love.

ॐ I choose to sanctify everyone I see.

ॐ I choose to share the light of love, the love of light with everyone. I choose to see it flowing between us, back and forth in an ongoing stream of blessedness.

INSPIRATION AND UPLIFTMENT

ॐ I intend to see every day as my new beginning, my New Jerusalem, my day of resurrection, and my springtime.

ॐ I intend to remember that the God of my life is a very present help in trouble.

ॐ I choose to remember on awakening that this is the day of my greatest opportunity for God's grace to manifest through me in my life.

ॐ I choose to allow the pain of separation to inspire the joy of reunion.

ॐ In the midst of trouble, I intend to be all right, because I'm moving through it.

ॐ I intend at all times to welcome the inspirations and helpful guidance from enlightened beings in all my endeavors.

ॐ I choose to acknowledge and imagine that help is on the way and always on time. By so doing, I include everything that is desirable.

ॐ I choose to remember that whatever I'm going through, no matter how painful, I am on my way Home.

ॐ I intend to experience a more expansive perception of life today than yesterday.

ॐ I choose to imagine the angel of change is sitting on my shoulder, lightening my burden through every change in my life.

ॐ I choose to focus on how I would feel if I were no longer in trouble.

ॐ I choose to remember that by the power of Soul, my life is getting better and better every day because the power of love is leading the way!

ॐ I choose to acknowledge that I am on the threshold of the next step of my evolution, of exploding awareness.

ॐ I choose to connect with the Divine within me, which is in charge, and all is very well indeed.

ॐ I intend at all times to call on the One within me that is greater than anything in the world.

ॐ I choose to remember the Divine in me unfolds in perfection all that concerns me at every level of my being—physically, emotionally, mentally, and spiritually.

ॐ I choose to acknowledge that the spirit of God goes before me to make my way harmonious and successful.

ॐ I intend to acknowledge at the beginning of any undertaking that God is where I am, and nothing is too hard for God to do and accomplish. Whatever God begins, God completes.

ॐ I choose to imagine that the Divine Mother covers me with her wings.

ॐ I intend to make this the best day of my life.

ॐ I intend to quench my thirst by drinking from the eternal spring of life, which is self-renewing.

ॐ I choose to remember that divine love inspires and guides me in all my thoughts, words, and actions.

ॐ I intend to acknowledge that love is the unfailing support and solution to every need and problem.

ॐ I choose to remember that my intention goes before me to make the crooked path straight.

ॐ I choose to treat myself by consulting my Inner Being for inspiration.

ॐ I choose to remember the Beloved gives His angels charge over me in all my ways.

INTUITION AND SELF-GUIDANCE

ॐ I intend to put love first in my life to inspire, empower, and guide me in all my decisions.

ॐ I intend to ask what love would have me do and to listen to the answer of my heart.

ॐ I intend to feel at all times that divine love is guiding me and anticipating everything that will make my life beautiful and allow me to grow and flourish.

ॐ I choose to acknowledge that I have the intuitive recognition of what is the best action to take each moment.

ॐ I intend to listen inwardly, paying close attention to the answer that is unfolding. I am feeling the rush of information catching up with me in the present.

ॐ I choose to be guided by the voice of love in every action, in everything I do, read, see, and hear.

ॐ I choose to hear only what the voice of intuition guides me to do.

ॐ I intend to be led to any resource that relates to my search.

ॐ My intention is to allow the answer to come in whatever way my Inner Being chooses.

ॐ I choose to welcome and celebrate inner guidance that responds beyond measure to my heart's pure desire.

ॐ I choose to entrust myself daily to inner guidance.

ॐ I choose to recognize intuitively the spiritual identity of every being.

ॐ I choose to meditate for guidance, knowing the answer is coming.

ॐ I intend at all times to be receptive to love's all-powerful, all-blissful, all-transforming guidance.

ॐ I choose to ask the Beloved to guide me to realize what will contribute to the greatest good. I remain open to His guidance from moment to moment.

ॐ I intend always to be listening inwardly for the guidance of my Inner Being. I choose to stay on the line. Beloved, speak and I will hear.

ॐ My intention is to pay attention to intuitive promptings no matter how faint they may be and to be still and ask: What is it I need to know in this moment?

ॐ I choose to be alert for God's will for me from moment to moment.

ॐ I intend to always listen inwardly for the guidance of my being, of God, of I Am.

ॐ I intend to let the Beloved of my heart commune with me and guide me in what to do.

ॐ I intend to remember there is no problem without the solution, and I welcome the solution by letting it in.

ॐ I intend to let my inner, wiser, intuitive Self guide my thoughts, words, desires, and actions at all times.

ॐ I choose to respond after asking my inner Self to show me what to say and what to do for my well-being and that of others.

ॐ I choose to seek the silence and wait upon the Lord.

ॐ I choose to listen to what the Beloved of my heart desires for me.

ॐ I choose to ask the Beloved to help me be totally receptive to His desire, will, love, and guidance.

ॐ I intend to follow the guidance of my voice of Soul and to let my senses be permeated with the love of Soul.

ॐ I choose to conduct myself in all my actions as though the Beloved were guiding my actions.

ॐ I request the universe to help me be open and receptive to whatever allows me to live in ever greater joy, freedom, and creative self-expression.

ॐ I choose to feel at ease as love guides me to the right place at the right time.

ॐ I choose to listen to what my heart would have me know that my mind cannot know.

ॐ My intention is to be constantly on the alert for insight.

ॐ I choose to act only under divine orders, only in conformity with the peace within me, only from the consciousness of love and right realization.

JOYFULNESS

ॐ I intend to live my life as a joyous adventure.

ॐ I choose to do everything in life that brings me joy.

ॐ I intend to grow in joy and to nurture every belief that contributes to my well-being and joy.

ॐ I choose and allow the feeling of joy to move through all my experiences to ever greater experiences of joy and well-being.

ॐ I choose to experience ever greater joy from moment to moment with total love.

ॐ I intend to include everyone in my experience of joy.

ॐ I choose my intentions with great joy.

ॐ I choose to enter into the joy of God, for God is my very being.

ॐ I intend to find the source of my joy and to discover it is ever new.

ॐ I choose to focus only on what is joy-bearing.

ॐ I intend to see how much more joy I can accommodate today. I give thanks for all the joy.

ॐ I intend to seek joy by facing Reality. If it doesn't bring me joy, then I am facing unreality.

ॐ I choose to focus within me on what is not limiting, for that is an unfailing source of joy.

ॐ I intend to grow in and through joy in all I do, for I am a joy-seeking being.

ॐ I choose to learn through joy.

ॐ I choose to remember that if I'm not experiencing joy, I am focusing on what doesn't bring joy.

ॐ I choose to recognize that nothing is more important than experiencing ongoing joy.

ॐ I choose to remain calm and undisturbed during suffering, because I go to joy.

ॐ I intend to find a million reasons for feeling supremely exuberant, joyful, and prosperous today.

ॐ I choose to delight and celebrate in life, singing a song unto the Lord.

ॐ I intend with clarity and loving consciousness to live in the joy of my being, no matter what I am experiencing.

ॐ I choose to speak only words that will bring me joy.

ॐ I eagerly and joyfully choose to welcome the next step in my journey for the greater experience of joy, wisdom, and love.

ॐ I intend to be an ever exuberant stream of self-renewal. I am willing to live in joy for God.

ॐ I intend to feel better and more joyful than what I'm feeling now.

ॐ I choose to move from joy to greater joy.

ॐ I choose to acknowledge that what will help me live intentionally is living joyfully.

ॐ I intend to continue unfolding joyfully and gratefully.

ॐ I choose, above all else, to experience and live in pure joy amidst all conditions, because joy is not dependent on what is happening around me.

ॐ It is my intention to perform all actions from the state of being that is called joy, from a loving state of being.

ॐ I choose to give my loving attention to experiencing joy in each moment.

ॐ I intend to express more and more joy each day.

LOVE

ॐ In the spaciousness of the heart, I choose to experience the never ending reality of love.

ॐ I intend wherever I am to welcome the stream of pure love, that it may flow freely through me to everyone and everything around me.

ॐ I intend to allow divine love to embody itself in my every thought, word, and action.

ॐ I intend to replace every unloving thought with a loving one.

ॐ I choose love to be my God, my guide, my teacher, my all.

ॐ I intend to let all of God's love circulate in my experience.

ॐ I intend to share the gift of unconditional love with everyone no matter how much it irks them or unsettles them, for love conquers all.

ॐ I choose to welcome any means that helps me love unconditionally from moment to moment.

ॐ I intend to cultivate only thoughts that flow to me on the current of divine love.

ॐ I choose to embody in fullness the love that is God.

ॐ I intend at all times to let love guide me in formulating my intentions.

ॐ I intend to love my enemy because it feels so good.

ॐ I intend to be true to the love that I Am under all circumstances.

ॐ I intend to experience lovingness in ever greater measure.

ॐ I choose to abide in the heart of the universe.

ॐ I choose to unfold the love that I Am.

ॐ I intend to love by initiating loving thoughts and identifying with lovely images and engaging in loving actions until everything I feel and do will be loving and lovely.

ॐ I intend to settle for nothing but the totality of love.

ॐ I intend to love as God loves, 24/7.

ॐ I intend to follow the light of love all the days of my life.

ॐ Every day, I choose to practice letting the power of love flow through me.

ॐ I intend to live my life as a loving being and to inspire everyone to love by asking God to show me how to do it.

ॐ I choose to experience the expression of divine love with everyone I meet.

ॐ I intend for love always to manifest in my life.

ॐ I intend to realize from moment to moment that I am born to express love and to share the fulfillment of love.

ॐ I intend to love equally friend and foe.

ॐ I choose to open myself to the universe of love and to experience God's love in fullness.

ॐ I choose to abide in the spirit, in the exuberance, in the vastness, in the manifestation of unconditional Self-love.

ॐ I choose to expand in unconditional love beyond all boundaries in consciousness.

ॐ I intend to make room in my busy schedule throughout the day to allow love to come in.

ॐ I choose to let my mind be so filled with love that it crowds out every other thought until nothing is left but the current of love, the ocean of Bliss.

ॐ I choose to let all my thoughts, actions, and relationships be guided by the love of the heart.

ॐ I choose to repeat the word "love" to myself and feel how it resonates.

ॐ I intend to find a way to expand my feelings of love until my love includes all creation.

ॐ I intend to be shown how to love everybody in as many ways as there are beings.

ॐ I intend to experience the expansiveness of love in action under all circumstances.

ॐ No matter what happens, I intend to feel the love that I Am working in and through me.

ॐ I choose to follow love wherever it takes me, knowing that love will only take me into greater love, greater appreciation, greater joy, greater freedom, and greater release from judgment of anyone.

ॐ I choose to behold all with the eye of love, for the eye of love is God beholding us as Itself.

ॐ I intend to let love teach me everything I need to know in a loving way.

ॐ I choose to focus on the love that is within me and to experience its activity in ever expanding circles of radiation.

ॐ I intend to acknowledge at all times that love precedes me, accompanies me, and returns to me.

ॐ In times of difficulty, I choose to remember there is nothing too difficult for divine love.

ॐ I choose to manifest love, to encounter love in as many ways as I can, as I take each breath today.

ॐ I choose to experience the power of divine love, the only power of the universe, as the all-sustaining, all-powerful, all-governing power in my life.

ॐ I choose to allow the love within me to remain undimmed by any human experiences.

ॐ I intend to make all decisions from the heart of love.

ॐ I choose to pour love into all my actions.

ॐ I intend to love everyone as God loves me.

ॐ I choose to act only in the consciousness of love and right-realization.

ॐ I choose to untie the knots of my heart.

ॐ I choose to let love lead, knowing the mind will follow.

ॐ I choose to purify my heart by filling it with the love of God.

ॐ I choose to see that all things are made of divine love.

ॐ I intend to love everyone with my heart and with my Soul by recognizing that everyone wants harmony, love, peace, and beauty.

ॐ I intend to remain loyal to supreme love by nurturing Self-love, the one Self in all.

ॐ I intend, Beloved, to listen to you, that you may transform my consciousness from limited to unlimited love.

ॐ I intend to experience the love of God and to let nothing else satisfy me any longer.

ॐ I choose to feel love pouring out through me without the need to explain it or advertise it and with no expectation of recognition.

ॐ I choose to nurture the love that I Am.

ॐ I choose to be in love with that which is love in everyone, knowing love blesses the one who is ready to love.

ॐ I intend to grow in love through all my experiences, which come and go; but I remain as love.

ॐ I choose to let all experiences reveal to me the presence of the love that is now ever present.

ॐ I choose to replace every judgment I have with the desire to love.

ॐ I choose to practice Self-love when love seems distant.

ॐ Every time I feel resistance to love, I choose to radiate more love.

ॐ I choose to perceive everything in life from the standpoint of unconditional love.

ॐ I intend to let go of every belief that does not support unconditional love.

ॐ I choose to do everything for love's sake.

ॐ I intend to dwell in the consciousness and feeling of unconditional love.

ॐ I choose to love because it feels so good.

ॐ I intend to let go of the disappointments of love to experience the power of unconditional love.

ॐ I intend to love God with all my heart, all my mind, my whole being.

ॐ I intend to acknowledge at all times that I am sustained by unconditional love.

ॐ I choose to summon and welcome the vibration of pure love.

ॐ I choose to dwell in the heart of the Beloved.

ॐ I enthusiastically intend to bring love and devotion into every self-expression, with every breath I take.

ॐ Whatever I do, I choose to find a way to do it with love.

ॐ I intend to have everything in my life go God's way, to be an expression of love.

ॐ I choose not to lower myself to another's standards, but to live by the standard of Self-love.

ॐ I choose love, which allows, inspires, and encourages me to see beyond appearances to that which love has to offer.

ॐ I choose to remember that I live in a world of love.

ॐ I choose to love and to allow the limitless to happen.

ॐ I intend to love everyone with the love of my Soul, which is ever pure.

🕉 I choose to rejoice that I have a desire to love unconditionally and that I can grow in that love.

🕉 I choose to remember that the love I Am is the love I share. I choose to find as many ways as possible to share that love.

🕉 I choose to love everyone as God loves, and I choose to be instructed by my own beloved Self as to how God loves me.

🕉 I intend at all times for my heart to be the abode of the Beloved, especially in the midst of appearances of duality.*

🕉 I intend to replace reality as man sees it with my own Reality, as love perceives Reality.

🕉 I choose to allow love to guide all my actions to loving results.

🕉 I intend to reflect before I act, to respond instead of reacting, to abide in the light and radiate within that light the spirit of oneness and love.**

🕉 I choose to love and to share the love that I Am, to manifest my true nature of love, and to find love manifesting in every experience.

🕉 I choose to know love, for love will heal my unknowingness.

🕉 As I take a deep breath, I intend to let love rush in to take care of all my activities. Thank you, Beloved of my heart.

🕉 I intend to put the love of God first before any undertaking.

🕉 I intend to merge my limited love with the infinite love of the Beloved within my heart.

🕉 I choose to know what unconditional love feels like and to enter into the joy of God, for God is my very being.

🕉 I choose to allow my mind to bow to the heart.

🕉 I choose to live my life in love, no matter what happens.

*Duality refers to polarities, such as pleasure and pain, good and bad, loss and gain, victory and defeat; duality also refers to the belief in ourselves as separate from God.

**Reaction is negative, whereas response is positive.

MEDITATION

ॐ I choose to experience an unbroken stream flowing to the Beloved.

ॐ I intend to merge with joy.

ॐ I intend to find that sacred place within me where there is no resistance to receiving only love.

ॐ I intend to love the silence, because the silence is my eternal friend and my mother. The silence reveals to me everything that contributes to my well-being, my sense of oneness.

ॐ I choose to be still and know the power of the silence, the center of my being from which comes omnipresent, omniscient, all-loving, all-inspiring, all-pure, ennobling thoughts, words, and deeds.

ॐ It is my passionate intention to follow the inner star of the East.

ॐ I intend to merge my limited love with the infinite love of the Beloved within my heart.

ॐ I intend to practice silent awareness for the joy of experiencing the power of silence.

ॐ I intend to merge my sense of separateness into the consciousness of unity.

ॐ O Beloved of my Soul, I choose to bathe in the ocean of thy love.

ॐ I choose to experience all that God is.

ॐ I intend to turn within and ponder what I need help with, what I want to change or to explore.

ॐ I intend for my mind to focus on that which takes me beyond all concepts.

ॐ I choose to recognize that the Self that I Am meditates in and through me.

ॐ I choose to imagine myself as the sun, radiating love into all dimensions.

ॐ I choose to focus my mind on the light of God at the spiritual eye and to merge with it.

ॐ I intend to merge my individual consciousness with Bliss-consciousness.

ॐ I choose to withdraw my attention from what's been demanding my attention and to focus on a crystalline stream of pure light floating through my mind.

ॐ I choose to enter into the inner chamber, lock my door, and pray to my Father in secret.

ॐ I intend to discover the beginning of all thought.

ॐ I intend to make a powerful connection with the source of wisdom, love, and manifestation.

ॐ I choose to be still, to be in a listening attitude.

ॐ I intend to meditate in order to forge greater links with the joy I seek to realize.

ॐ I choose to make all my distractions a part of the divine attraction.

ॐ I choose to be in the state of stillness, of receptivity to God's grace and guidance.

ॐ I choose to rise above all thought and be bathed in the Bliss of being.

ॐ I intend to meditate with powerful commitment to listen to the Beloved guiding me from moment to moment.

ॐ I choose to ask the Beloved to draw me unto Itself, beyond thought, word, and speech, where there is only love flowing between us.

ॐ I intend to offer every distraction to the Lord of my being.

ॐ I choose to meditate with the intent of forging more powerful links with the Source, which brings me greater light, love, and desire to know my Self and realize my oneness with all.

ॐ I choose to experience the quietness of mind.

ॐ I choose to turn within to the Beloved of my heart, who alone is my support and strength.

ॐ I choose to allow God to meditate Its vision through me.

ONENESS

ॐ I choose to abide in the consciousness of oneness in all circumstances, which is to abide in Self-love.

ॐ I choose to make my heart the guest room for all sojourning travelers.

ॐ My intention is to feel the presence and activity of wholeness in the midst of its opposition.

ॐ I choose to realize that with love there is only wholeness, or oneness.

ॐ I intend to see everyone with the eyes of God—as beautiful and whole, and with the eyes of love.

ॐ I choose to welcome and celebrate the beloved Father in all beings.

ॐ I intend to see beyond all forms to the love that made them all.

ॐ I intend to connect with all beings who share my love of connectedness with the Earth.

ॐ I choose to reach out in compassion, for it is love in action.

ॐ I choose to acknowledge my oneness with the Source.

ॐ I intend to remain loyal to supreme love by nurturing Self-love, the one Self in all.

ॐ I choose to use my eyes to perceive the light of God in all creation and created, in all beings and undulations of life.

ॐ I intend to feel oneness with everyone every day.

ॐ I choose to love the one Spirit and celebrate its wholeness.

ॐ I choose to relate to another in oneness because I perceive myself as the other.

ॐ I choose to behold each person in his or her Soul-light at the spiritual center and feel myself merging with it.

ॐ I choose to be aligned only with that which is the divinity of all.

ॐ With everyone, I choose to remember, "You are with me in the heart of God."

PASSION

ॐ I choose to live my whole day with enthusiasm, because life is crammed full of God's presence.

ॐ Every day I choose to give of myself passionately on all levels, knowing the joy of doing so feels delightful.

ॐ I choose to experience the fullness of life.

ॐ I choose nonresistance to experiencing the totality of life.

ॐ I choose to be on a rampage of experiencing powerful enthusiasm by seeing God in everyone and every activity.

ॐ I choose to feel passion for the well-being of (name of person) in the midst of sorrow, alienation, and loneliness.

ॐ I choose to experience continuous unfoldment and the magnificence of the Self in an ever expanding universe.

ॐ I choose to go forth, willing to experience the fullness of the journey.

ॐ I choose to welcome all desire as part of my self-unfoldment and growth in spiritual awareness.

ॐ I choose to realize more of limitless love, universal oneness, joyful living, and abundant livelihood.

ॐ I intend to fall in love with my heart's desire until it becomes an all-consuming fire and I become the embodiment of God's love, light, spirit, bliss, grace, and abundance.

PEACE AND HARMONY

🕉 I choose to focus only on that which brings me peace of mind.

🕉 I choose to be centered in the consciousness of peace, regardless of what is happening around me.

🕉 I choose to acknowledge the peace within you.

🕉 I choose to live in the consciousness of peace, knowing no problem can overcome me.

🕉 I choose to be a center of peace wherever I am, wherever God places me.

🕉 I choose to allow unconditional love to conquer all without making war.

🕉 It is my intention to live in a state of balance and harmony. I choose to relate to the world from this place of harmony.

🕉 I choose to see my enemy as my potential friend.

🕉 My intention is to love my enemy as the enlightened ones love.

🕉 I intend to experience the power of peace in my life.

ॐ I intend each day to commune with the center of peace within me, that I may perform all actions in the consciousness of peace.

ॐ I choose eagerly and joyfully to be a radiator of peace.

ॐ I choose to share peace for the benefit of the whole world.

ॐ I choose to find harmony within myself, knowing I will find harmony in the world.

ॐ I choose to reassociate with the source of peace.

ॐ I choose to cauterize every negative emotion within myself, that I may fully know peace within.

ॐ I choose to be a peacemaker by forgiving everyone in this world.

ॐ I choose to remember that right where I am, God has left His peace with me. He is always with me.

ॐ I choose to accept everything as it is with a peaceful state of mind.

ॐ I choose to practice total self-forgiveness in order to know peace.

ॐ I choose to act only in conformity with the center of peace within me.

ॐ I intend to sleep in peace and to awake in peace and harmony.

PLAYFULNESS

ॐ I choose to see whatever I see in a way that brings lightness and gladness of heart.

ॐ I intend to have fun doing whatever I do, and I look forward to doing whatever I did not get done.

ॐ I intend to allow playfulness in my experience, regardless of how humanly important or serious an endeavor or perception would appear to be.

ॐ I choose to remember that life is a game, and I'm going to have fun.

ॐ I choose to enter into everything that I do with a playful spirit.

ॐ I intend to have fun with the roles I play.

ॐ I choose to give life a chance and I will dance.

ॐ I choose to answer the call of life playfully and to move beyond strife.

ॐ I choose to have fun regaining the kingdom of my true Self.

ॐ I choose to remember that spirituality is having fun with life.

ॐ My intention is to live in the spontaneity and playfulness of divine love.

ॐ I choose to milk every moment for all the fun I can have.

POSITIVE THOUGHT

ॐ I choose to have a positive attitude under all circumstances.

ॐ I intend to make the best of each experience.

ॐ I intend to occupy my mind with thoughts that are uplifting, with feelings that are healing, and with perceptions that are liberating.

ॐ I intend to be a transmitter of love and light and creative ideas.

ॐ I intend to anticipate having many wonderful experiences today, because it's a pact I have made with myself.

ॐ I intend to remember that it's a good thing to be where I am in my journey.

ॐ I choose to embrace change, for it brings greater opportunities for growth.

ॐ I intend to focus only on that which is fruitful in a positive way and keeps me moving in my appreciation.

ॐ I choose to shift my focus from the problem to the solution.

ॐ I choose to be on a rampage of positive thinking, to let my light shine.

🕉 I choose to look for the best, knowing that I will always experience the best.

🕉 I choose to begin every day by seeing the best in everything and everyone and to do my best through unconditional love.

🕉 I intend to share more and more light.

🕉 I choose to let positive thoughts merge with positive feelings and to bear witness to the birth of spiritual fulfillment.

🕉 By the power of Soul, I choose to feel my life is getting better and better every day because the power of love is leading the way!

🕉 I intend to enjoy my destiny while I am here.

RELATIONSHIPS

ॐ I choose to be loving, understanding, kind, and playful in all my relationships.

ॐ I intend always to remember that the love in my heart is vast enough to accommodate a different viewpoint, attitude, or belief.

ॐ In every relationship, my intention is to increase my realization of love.

ॐ I choose to love everyone whether they like it or not.

ॐ When seeming differences arise with another, I intend to offer mutual respect, unconditional love, joy, and playfulness.

ॐ I choose to respond with love instead of reacting, for nothing on the outside has power over me.

ॐ I choose to love others because Love has loved me first.

ॐ When I have difficulties seeing others as God sees them, I choose to request the God of my being to show me what it is like to perceive His creations the way He does, because that is what I'd love to do.

ॐ I choose to remember that love always finds a way because love always knows how to relate.

ॐ I choose to cultivate the spirit of benevolence in all my relationships.

ॐ I choose never to take sides, because love includes all sides and aspects.

ॐ I choose to connect with the master within who does not interact with another's negativity.

ॐ I choose to see the creative, loving potential of every being.

ॐ I intend to expand so fully with the supportiveness of love that wherever I am placed, I can express that love in every interaction.

ॐ I choose to see the stream of love filling all of my consciousness, which includes the other with whom I am relating.

ॐ I choose now to focus only on how another would feel if he or she was filled with Self-love.

ॐ I intend to be open to love with everyone.

ॐ I choose to focus on the love that I Am, which opens me to feeling the love of another.

ॐ I choose to remember that the only enemy I have to love is myself.

༃ I intend to suspend all judgment so that I may experience a greater measure of love.

༃ In all my relationships, I intend to recognize what unites us, what we have in common—the Source within us that guides us to the healing power of love.

༃ I choose always to see others at their best and to magnify and acknowledge their divinity, their original state of wholeness.

༃ I intend to apply the truths of prayer in all my relationships throughout the day.

༃ I choose to perceive everything in my relationships from the standpoint of unconditional love.

༃ I intend in all my relationships and encounters to exercise spiritual discernment to guide me in the proper response.

༃ I choose to love everyone in the midst of all they are doing.

༃ I choose to respond with a loving heart and with the best in myself.

༃ I intend to remember that even the most wretched and deprived human being contains the seed of divinity. I bow to that divinity.

ॐ I choose to remember that First Love, the love of God, is the only love that can fulfill me.

ॐ I choose to stay with the nobility of divine nature, no matter what names I am called.

ॐ When I feel upset with another, I choose to focus on one quality of this person I can love.

ॐ Instead of judging according to appearances, I choose to acknowledge the other's strengths.

ॐ I intend to see everyone as my friend, because no one is to blame.

ॐ I choose to soothe another's pain by understanding the cause of that pain and to embrace the other in my heart (as the mother holds her crying child when it has been hurt or feels lonely).

ॐ I intend to replace judgment with understanding. Every time I am tempted to judge, I choose love.

ॐ Whenever a person comes to my mind, I choose to see that person at his or her best at all times.

RELEASING NEGATIVE EMOTIONS

ॐ I intend to renounce every form of anger, because love and well-being feel so much more empowering, rewarding, and fulfilling than remaining in anger.

ॐ I intend in my quiet moments to get to the root of my self-inflicted anger so I may free myself of it. That which I project, I inflict on myself.

ॐ In the midst of what bothers me, I choose to focus on what doesn't bother me.

ॐ I intend to find something to feel good about in the midst of my anger, something that feels better than anger.

ॐ I intend to be alert to any discomfort I feel about anything and immediately choose what feels better by focusing on what feels better.

ॐ I choose not to personalize anything I don't want to experience.

ॐ I intend at all times to overcome all negativity—fear, anger, blame, shame, guilt, sadness, worry, or grief—by calling into being the feeling that equates with self-empowerment.

ॐ I choose to remember that I have a choice whether to focus on fear or on love.

🕉 I choose and allow myself to move through any feeling of discomfort and discordance by appreciating the gift of insight and creative ideas, and I choose to let self-expansion dominate.

🕉 I choose to focus on the most important thing for me to feel in the midst of this experience.

🕉 Whenever I observe or experience any form of anxiety or fear, I choose to remember that I belong to divine love.

🕉 I choose to experience what is present in the absence of fear.

🕉 Whenever I feel the need for self-glorification, I choose to acknowledge I already have all of God's glory, and I give glory to God for all things.

🕉 I intend to let go of all self-blame, shame, guilt, condemnation, or judgment of anything I have done, said, or experienced within myself or with others.

🕉 I choose to let my attention go only to where there is a feeling of security.

🕉 When I feel upset or angry, I choose to ask myself how much longer I want to feel this way.

🕉 I choose to reframe any experience that feels negative.

ॐ I choose to face my fear and, by doing so, to realize I am greater than the fear.

ॐ I choose to move beyond the obstacles that keep me from experiencing God's grace.

ॐ I choose to live my life of love no matter how terrible I feel.

ॐ I choose to reconcile myself with change so that I will let go of grief and have peace of mind.

ॐ I choose to continue transforming old habits and patterns, because I choose the habit of well-being.

ॐ When I feel overwhelmed, I choose to ask: What would love do in the midst of this experience?

ॐ I choose to feel better than I've been feeling.

ॐ I choose to focus on the one feeling I'd like to have all day long.

ॐ I choose to renounce any resistance to well-being.

ॐ I choose to go beyond my history and fragmented past to my spirituality, my wholeness.

ॐ I intend to surrender all my weaknesses to the one power of love.

ॐ When joy, peace, harmony, and love are not present,
I choose to ask: What is present in my mind when I am
not in a state of well-being?

ॐ I choose to rise above any negativity.

ॐ I choose to feast on that which would be present if there
were no negative images.

ॐ I choose to leave any enmity or negative thoughts behind
when I approach the altar of my heart.

ॐ I intend to remember that nothing will help me overcome
worry like going to the center of love.

ॐ I intend to shatter the habit of blame, judgment, and fear
by focusing on their opposites till the opposites are
transformed into my total identity.

ॐ I choose to acknowledge my pain and then ask what it
has to teach me.

ॐ In the midst of anger, loneliness, fear, insecurity, or pain,
I choose to love myself.

ॐ I choose to observe the pain and remember that which
I Am in the present is greater than that which I am
aware of in the present.

ॐ The moment a negative experience comes up on my radar screen, I choose to charge it with light, and it cannot stay in my awareness.

ॐ I choose to behold any negative condition only momentarily. If I dwell on it, it is mine.

ॐ I choose to practice reviewing my moods and attitudes, and to ask: On a scale of 1–10, where would my negative output be? What would feel better?

ॐ I choose to remember that the way I move beyond negative habits is to move into total appreciation for what I have.

ॐ I choose to connect with the Beloved of my being by seeing God on the altar of my heart and bringing to the Beloved all my feelings of fear, anger, hurt, appreciation, and joy.

ॐ I choose to be receptive to the memories from my childhood that help me gain a greater understanding of what happened, so I can share that understanding for the good of others.

ॐ I choose to remember that any negative emotion shows me I am not feeling the presence of God. I choose to breathe deeply and connect with God's presence.

ॐ I choose to no longer believe that I have to be the victim of any negative thought or emotion.

ॐ I choose to let go of all thoughts that do not contribute to my well-being.

ॐ I choose to remember that help is always present and available. No emotion has power over me.

ॐ I choose to replace any negative or painful feeling with the love that is unconditional.

ॐ I choose to supplant the negative thought or emotion I had with one that I choose to experience until I feel well-being.

ॐ I choose to remember that it takes practice to develop negative habits, and it takes practice to develop my new, healthy habits.

ॐ I choose to focus on anything that makes me feel better.

ॐ I choose to remain in the divine presence as I observe the passage of the wave of emotion.

SELF-ACCEPTANCE AND SELF-WORTH

ॐ I choose to nurture the love that I Am.

ॐ I choose to shift my focus from making a mistake to putting love into action.

ॐ I choose to love myself 100 percent.

ॐ I choose to embrace myself by embracing the love that I Am.

ॐ I choose to remember that love is always waiting for me when my heart hurts.

ॐ I choose to remember that I am forever loved by the Beloved, no matter how much forgetfulness I generate to maintain a sense of separateness to justify my resistance.

ॐ I intend to use every so-called failure to inspire greater success.

ॐ I choose to love myself so much that nothing but love radiates through me to others.

ॐ I choose to become a magnet of Self-appreciation and to attract all that is Self-appreciating.

ॐ I intend to expand in Self-love, that I may realize my limitlessness and the beauty and perfection of creation and created.

ॐ In my desire to express unconditional love, I choose to accept all aspects of myself.

ॐ I choose to look through the mirror and identify with the love that shines through my eyes.

ॐ I choose to remember that I belong to God, to infinite love, not to anyone else.

ॐ I choose to rejoice in who I Am, to find something within me that causes me to rejoice.

ॐ I intend to free myself of the struggle to be pure by choosing to remain open to God's grace and to be dedicated to do everything with love.

ॐ In the midst of feeling unworthy, I choose to move beyond this feeling of unworthiness.

ॐ I choose to remember that only infinite love can fulfill my longing.

ॐ I choose to remember that I do not have to suffer because I made someone else suffer.

ॐ I choose to focus only on noble qualities, for when I do, I feel a healthy self-esteem.

ॐ I choose to remember that I live in a universe of total love and support.

ॐ I choose to be loving and kind to myself; this makes me loving to others.

ॐ I intend to pamper myself with divine thought.

ॐ I choose to honor and remember the purpose of my life.

ॐ I choose to call unto myself whatever divine qualities are necessary to companion me.

ॐ This day I intend to experience greater supportiveness of myself.

ॐ I choose to remember that I am the Beloved's forever, and therefore I am always loved and provided for unconditionally.

ॐ I choose to see myself as God sees me.

ॐ I choose to treat myself as I want to be treated and as I want to treat others.

ॐ Where I have held onto unforgivingness, I am resolved to give love to myself to love the pain away.

ॐ I choose to love myself as God loves me and to be instructed by my own beloved Self as to how God loves me.

ॐ I choose to heal my perception of myself, which heals my perception of others.

ॐ I choose to connect with the stream of well-being no matter where I am and what I am doing.

ॐ I choose to remember: That which is within me is the love that will never let me go.

ॐ I choose to remember that security is knowing who I Am and loving myself unconditionally.

ॐ I choose to accept my innate divinity of absolute perfection.

ॐ I choose to remember that, in the eyes of love, I am most precious and eternally loved.

ॐ I choose to love myself in the midst of all that happens.

ॐ On the way to enlightenment, I choose to remember not to take anyone's judgment personally, not even my own.

ॐ I choose to love my misperception and allow it to be what it is.

ॐ I intend to remember that which I Am looks out through these two eyes and does not judge me for anything I experience.

ॐ I intend to remember that love is always waiting for me within.

ॐ I choose to remember that God's image of me is always one of wholeness, joy, and oneness.

ॐ I choose to honor the level of life education I've experienced, which helps me grow to the next level.

ॐ I intend to remember: It is my divine birthright to flourish, to live in freedom, to experience the glory of God, the love of God in action, because God sees me as God sees Itself—as divine.

ॐ I choose to give thanks for the love that I Am, which gives me discernment to recognize conditioning and to create new and better conditions with my loving attention.

ॐ I choose to give my inner child what my parents could not give.

ॐ For every fault I find within myself, I intend to find something I appreciate within myself.

ॐ I choose to overcome every resistance to unconditional love within myself.

ॐ By the grace of the Beloved, I choose to perceive the best that exists in me, that manifests through me and flows out from me to everyone I see.

ॐ I choose to remember there are no obstacles to loving God, except one: not loving myself. Therefore, I choose every day to love myself the way God loves me.

ॐ I choose to see myself clothed in a garment of pure light energy, custom-tailored for my specific needs.

ॐ I intend to rejoice in this ongoing journey of learning more about myself without any need to apologize.

ॐ I choose to remember that when I see the best in myself, I have the capacity to love others.

ॐ I choose to realize that I have come as the extension of infinite love to manifest and experience love on Earth for the mutual benefit of all.

ॐ I intend to manifest more self-love by allowing the love that I Am to manifest with wisdom and power, purity and joy on all levels of my being.

ॐ I intend to remember at all times that I am love, otherwise I could not choose to love. I could not love myself if I were not love.

ॐ I intend to look for countless reasons to express appreciation for who I Am, the love that I Am, and to recognize the love in all beings that is their true identity.

SELF-EMPOWERMENT

ༀ I choose to take total responsibility for every thought, feeling, desire, and action.

ༀ I intend to be transformed by the application of every intention.

ༀ I choose to be master of the moment.

ༀ From moment to moment, I choose to have absolute certainty that I can choose what I am experiencing next.

ༀ I intend to change my reality of self-imposed limitations and judgments to a new reality that expresses my innate nature of unconditional love, wisdom, well-being, abundance, and blissfulness.

ༀ I am empowered to see through the karmic pattern regarding betrayal and its consequences weaving itself like a thread through many lifetimes. I choose to detach myself from this thread.

ༀ I choose to bear witness to the power of self-transformation by the renewing of my mind from moment to moment.

ༀ If I don't feel happy being who I am, I choose to get myself out of the way.

ॐ I choose to be willing to overcome my unsupportive habits.

ॐ I choose to no longer justify my reason for doing anything.

ॐ I choose to change all inner conversations that are not
pleasing to hear.

ॐ When I'm not happy with my work, I choose to change
my attitude toward it.

ॐ I choose not to be diverted from honoring what I came
to do.

ॐ I intend to remember that God is in the driver's seat
wherever I go.

ॐ I choose to expand in consciousness beyond the limitations
that I feel.

ॐ I intend to reclaim my God-given spiritual dominion
over all thoughts, habits, and beliefs that come into
my awareness.

ॐ I intend to make it a habit to go back to the time I didn't
have the unsupportive habit.

ॐ I choose to remember that no one can prevent me from
experiencing love and joy.

ॐ I choose to remember that, in the moment, I have all the power to change my conditioning (patterns), for conditioning is limited.

ॐ I choose to give my attention only to that which makes me happy.

ॐ I choose to breathe, live, and love the feeling of success and victory in all my endeavors.

ॐ I intend to remain open to whatever is helpful to my journey of ever greater Self-unfoldment.

ॐ I intend to go forth bearing the shield of light to deflect anything that is not the light.

ॐ I intend to use everything I learn to show me the next step in unfolding ever greater insight and understanding.

ॐ I take a vow that never again will I expect another human being to be responsible for my happiness, freedom, well-being, success, peace, or growth; for I am the manifestor and attractor of all I experience. I Am.

ॐ I intend to discover better or more beneficial ways to do what I have been doing.

ॐ I intend to remember that whatever I conceive myself to be, I become. I am the creator of my experiences.

ॐ I use everything I learn to help me take the next step in this ongoing journey of learning more and more about myself and what contributes magnificently to my well-being.

ॐ I choose to remember that my consciousness is the creator of everything that comes into my life.

ॐ I intend to please others only if it is also pleasing to myself.

ॐ I intend to transform every failure into a stepping stone to greater success.

ॐ I choose to remember that wherever I am, I am the one choosing to identify with whatever is happening.

ॐ I choose to change my future in the present.

ॐ I intend at all times to be consciously aware of what I accept into my consciousness and what I do not accept.

ॐ I choose to remember that my life is powerful enough to support all changes.

ॐ I choose to invest my attention, time, and service in only that which I love to experience.

ॐ I intend to succeed in everything I love to do.

ॐ I intend to honor and respect my friends, but I am not controlled by their desires, wishes, or preferences.

ॐ I choose to be responsible for my perceptions, my interpretations of my perceptions, and what I project.

ॐ I choose to experience continuous unfoldment and the magnificence of myself in an ever expanding universe.

ॐ I choose to remember that conditions do not shape my life; my life shapes my conditions.

ॐ I choose to remember that my consciousness is the creator of everything that comes into my life.

ॐ I vow to expect the best of myself at all times and not to expect anything from another.

ॐ I choose not to allow anyone ever again to determine for me how I feel.

ॐ I choose to remember that no amount of conditioning can deny my spiritual heritage.

ॐ I choose to remember that others can guide me, but it is up to me to take the steps.

ॐ I choose to know at the very core of my being that I can, with powerful, passionate, clear intention, activate the change in any previously established pattern in the present moment.

ॐ I intend to be transformed by the application of every intention. I give thanks in advance for their fulfillment in the resurrection of my spiritual identity and unconditional love.

SELF-ENERGIZING

ॐ I intend to feel exuberant and energized regardless of where I am and what I am doing.

ॐ I choose to realize that I am the energy that energizes my thoughts.

ॐ I choose to remember that I have all the energy and time I need to accomplish what I want, love, and need to do.

ॐ I choose to dwell in the heart, the secret place of the Most High, where I feel the activation of blessed energy flowing through me.

ॐ I choose to focus on having all the energy I could possibly manifest.

ॐ I choose joy in knowing I will never get it done because life is infinite.

ॐ I choose to breathe the spirit of life into that which needs energizing.

ॐ I choose to remember that God is the inexhaustible source of the energy of my life.

ॐ I choose to remember that I do not lack energy, just the knowledge of how to connect with it.

ॐ I intend to remember that when I use energy, I always have more. Energy is never limited to an external activity.

ॐ I intend to caress each of the following words for 30 seconds or more throughout the day to energize myself and to become aware of their vibration:
- ~ Joy
- ~ Love
- ~ Sharing
- ~ Delight
- ~ Expansion
- ~ Optimism

SELF-REALIZATION

ॐ I choose to live in God-consciousness.

ॐ I choose to return to the source of being.

ॐ I intend to magnify and glorify my divine attributes.

ॐ I intend to allow the power of God-consciousness to flow through me consistently.

ॐ I choose to feast on that which I Am.

ॐ I choose to participate fully in God's will and to allow it to be expressed through me.

ॐ I choose to remember at all times who I Am.

ॐ I choose, Beloved, to feel thy love in waking, eating, serving, speaking, loving, living, intentioning, creating, manifesting, and meditating.

ॐ I intend to remember my holiness under all circumstances.

ॐ I choose at all times to see as God sees, to love as God loves, to be open of mind and expansive of heart so that the light of wisdom and the power of love can flow through me without obstruction and go wherever they are called to go.

ॐ I choose to bear witness to the Father who has sent me.

ॐ I choose to realize God's will in everything—the loving, manifesting power of my creative, infinite consciousness.

ॐ I intend to realize that the glory of God abides within me.

ॐ I choose to do something beautiful for God.

ॐ I choose to remember I am a stream of pure consciousness, the divine living itself through me.

ॐ I choose to experience the blessing of my own nature, which is divine and unconditionally loving.

ॐ I intend to expand in my knowledge, my realization of "I Am that I Am."

ॐ I choose to rest in the realization that my heart is pure, for the Beloved dwells in my heart.

ॐ I choose to realize that every action is an opportunity to acknowledge the sacredness of life, God acting through me.

ॐ I choose to make my heart an altar, a sanctuary.

ॐ I choose to ask God to think Its thoughts through me.

ॐ I intend to share the love that I Am, that others may realize the love that they are.

ॐ I intend to enjoy the feeling of the divine moving through me in full awareness.

ॐ I choose to unfold my consciousness into ever greater states of consciousness.

ॐ I intend to experience more fully each day a greater measure of the Infinite.

ॐ My intention is to follow my ideal, my supreme purpose.

ॐ My intention is to take great joy in the unfoldment of perfection for myself and all beings.

ॐ I intend to continue unfolding the magnificence that is the Self.

ॐ I choose to remember that the I of me is total love. It is ever expanding and replenishing me on all levels.

ॐ I choose to remember that I and my Father are one, because there is only infinity.

ॐ I choose to follow the light of my ideal with steadfast love, knowing I will succeed in manifesting and sharing it.

ॐ I behold and rejoice that I Am, making all things new.

ॐ I choose to love my Self into the feeling of fulfillment.

ॐ I choose to be willing to recognize the magnificence of who I Am.

ॐ I choose to focus on the polestar of my life, the most blessed thought, ideal, and desire that keeps me on course.

ॐ I choose to vibrate with the love that I Am.

ॐ From the moment of awakening, I choose to remember my true nature is the nature of God, expressing in the name "I Am."

ॐ I am determined to let nothing come between me and my love for God.

ॐ I choose to live a spiritual life, one that is joyful, creative, expansive, all-forgiving.

ॐ I choose to remember the purpose of my life is to manifest my divinity on earth.

ॐ I choose to dwell on aspects of my divinity until they become the substance of my consciousness.

ॐ I intend that every time I say "I Am," I will glorify the presence of God.

ॐ I choose to remember that every face is the face of God.

ॐ I choose to renounce the arrogance of believing myself to be less than God.

ॐ I intend to replace reality as man sees it with my own Reality, as love perceives Reality.

ॐ I choose to give glory to my divine nature, which is God.

ॐ I choose to immerse myself totally in what I choose to realize.

ॐ I choose to identify with my divine nature.

ॐ I choose to remember that Self-realization depends on myself, not on someone else.

ॐ I choose to remember the difference between who I Am and what I experience. This is Self-realization.

ॐ I intend to be aligned only with my innate divinity, which is one with the divinity of all.

ॐ I choose to imagine that my eyes are God's eyes.

ॐ It is my clear, passionate, powerful intention to channel every thought, belief, desire, and attitude into the stream of pure consciousness to merge into the ocean of bliss.

ॐ I choose to stay consciously connected to the source of all manifestations.

ॐ I intend, Beloved, to be molten in thy love and to see all
my actions as streams of light, merging into thy ocean
of bliss.

ॐ I intend to experience the power of divine love, the only
power of the universe, as the all-sustaining, all-powerful,
all-governing power in my life.

ॐ I choose to be in God-consciousness, to be filled with
the love of God.

ॐ I choose to realize that I Am the grace of God. Therefore
I can choose to experience the grace of my being forever.

ॐ I choose to remember that I am only fulfilled when I
know and express who I Am.

ॐ I intend to stay connected with the sacredness of my being.

ॐ I choose, Beloved, to allow to flow through my mind,
my heart, my senses, and my body-temple all of your
wisdom, your love, your light, your healing power, your
grace, your joy, your bliss, your energy, your vitality,
your inspiration, your creative ideas, your visions for me
and for your world.

ॐ I intend to intensify my longing for thee, until the last
shred of resistance to thy love disappears into nothingness,
into divine brilliance.

ॐ I choose to take the mind to its limits and come to the heart.

ॐ I choose to establish my mind and heart on the Beloved One.

ॐ It is my intention to participate fully in this divine adventure of Self-enlightenment, of growing in unconditional love.

ॐ I choose to remember that the grace of divine love is my sufficiency in all things, for it is the substance of all forms and assumes whatever form and experience is needed to assist me in remembering that I am the expression of God's grace when I live by God's grace.

ॐ I intend to remember that the Christ dwells within me as the eternal power of love and wisdom.

ॐ I rejoice in my ability to let all my desires merge in my supreme desire.

ॐ It is my clear, passionate, powerful intention to perform all actions in the consciousness of the universal Self.

ॐ I choose to know the true nature of the Beloved, in whose eyes my every thought, word, and movement are always beautiful.

ॐ I choose to assume the reality of that which I choose to be.

ॐ I choose to remember that the best place for me to realize God is where I am.

ॐ I choose to remember that everything is the manifestation of God.

ॐ I choose to remember that my divine connection is sound, eternal, and intact.

ॐ I choose to experience enlightenment from moment to moment.

ॐ I choose to live in the light that has guided me throughout eternity.

ॐ I choose to remember that the life of God speaks through me, so that when I speak, only God's word is heard.

ॐ I choose to turn to the secret place of the Most High within me.

ॐ I intend to be alive to the effects of my inner life on my world of experience.

ॐ I choose to change every worldly hope into a spiritual aspiration.

ॐ I invite the wisdom of the Divine Mother to illumine my path.

ॐ I choose to realize that I Am the One that is forever one with all that manifests.

SERVICE

ॐ I choose to remember that my purpose in life is to express love through service.

ॐ I choose to devote my life to acts of service and love with gratitude.

ॐ I choose to be of service, for this keeps me focused on what loves and heals.

ॐ I choose and love to be where I can be most effective.

ॐ I intend to support everyone in his or her journey.

ॐ I choose to thank the Father within me every time I am able to do anything for another.

ॐ I choose to remember that the Father within me doeth the work.

ॐ I choose to sanctify everything I do, for I do everything for the upliftment of all.

ॐ By the grace of the Beloved, I choose to be guided to bring joy and service into my every action and activity.

ॐ By the grace of the Beloved, I choose to behold others experiencing the benefit of the love I allow to flow through me in thought, word, and service.

ॐ I choose to work with loving attention to whatever presents itself to me each moment, but I will not be a slave to what I do or to anyone else who thinks he is the doer.

ॐ By the grace of the Beloved, I choose to realize I am blessed with infinite opportunity to render service and to stay in the flow of divine abundance.

ॐ By the grace of the Beloved, I choose to realize my endeavors bear boundless fruitage and blessings.

ॐ I choose to feast on how I would feel when I am able to be of service to another.

ॐ I choose to remember that of my own self, I can do nothing.

ॐ I intend to see my work in a new way each day.

ॐ I intend to remember that all praise goes to the divine, which works through me.

ॐ I intend to find ever better ways to express my love through service.

ॐ I choose for everything I do to benefit everyone.

ॐ I choose to remember that the moment I attempt to glorify myself, my light is dimmed, so I choose to glorify the Beloved of all actions.

ॐ I intend to extend my love and service to everyone, to share that which I know and love with no strings attached.

ॐ I intend to let God guide everyone who benefits from the services I offer and to be richly blessed by doing so.

ॐ I choose to allow God's grace, love, and abundance to flow through me on behalf of others.

ॐ I choose to have the Father-Mother God use me to share my gifts—my joy, love, healing, and strength—with everyone.

ॐ I intend to let my light shine, for it is the light of love shining in me and through me.

ॐ Every time I complete a task, I choose to ask the Beloved, "What would you have me do next?"

ॐ I intend to ask the Beloved to use me in whatever way would be healing to the world.

ॐ I choose to serve divinity with gladness.

ॐ I choose to remember the spirit of love is always with me, guiding me, supporting me, and sustaining me in all my unselfish actions.

ॐ I choose to be an instrument, the mouthpiece of the divine, and to speak only when the divine mouth has something to say.

ॐ I choose to put God first in action, for when I do, I render service and am filled with joy, love, and gratitude.

ॐ I choose to serve the divine spark in everyone.

ॐ I choose to call on the almighty source of wisdom within me to guide my thoughts, feelings, and perceptions so that I will be guided to do what is helpful.

ॐ I choose to invite the spirit of God—wisdom, truth, love, and peace—to fill me to overflowing to bless all those I meet.

ॐ I intend to experience God's loving will for me as an expression of itself in service every day.

ॐ I choose to remember that when I offer loving service, not just when there is a great need but as an expression of who I Am, the whole universe benefits.

ॐ I choose to remember that service is doing my best from moment to moment.

ॐ I intend to remember at all times who is the doer, no matter how I feel.

॰ॐ I choose to dedicate my "I" to promoting well-being, enlightenment, freedom, creativity, and joy for myself and everyone.

॰ॐ It is my intention to be open and receptive to divine grace in whatever form it takes in my life, that I may be a blessing to everyone.

॰ॐ I intend with great love and joy to cultivate whatever talent I have, that it may bless my life and the life of everyone.

॰ॐ I choose to be in a state of receptivity to allow divine qualities to manifest through me in loving service.

॰ॐ I choose to move from service to greater service.

॰ॐ I intend to experience so much bliss that I can help others experience bliss.

॰ॐ I choose to claim my divine birthright to grow through love, with the understanding that service is my relationship with all of life.

॰ॐ I intend to be awake, alert, and ready to respond to every need with integrity and mutual benefit.

॰ॐ I choose to focus on the gifts that I have brought with me into this life and to share them.

ॐ I choose to be in the state of receptivity, to allow God's qualities to manifest through me in loving service.

ॐ I choose to remember that I cannot raise a finger without God raising it.

ॐ I choose to share the beauty, the light, the magnificence, the gift of life that I Am and have to share.

ॐ I intend to be a transmitter of love and light and creative ideas.

ॐ I choose to manifest my divinity on Earth and to share it with others.

ॐ I intend to offer worship in everything I do by recognizing that God is the doer.

ॐ I choose to allow the love that I Am constantly to emit blessings upon all forms and activities of life.

ॐ I choose to be alert to God's will for me from moment to moment.

TRUTH

🕉 I intend to connect with the light of truth, which always meets my every need.

🕉 I intend to welcome truth in whatever way it may come.

🕉 I choose to rejoice in the gift of truth.

🕉 I choose to remember that truth is my shield and buckler.

🕉 I intend to remind myself that truth is not difficult to know. What is not easy is letting go of untruth.

🕉 I fearlessly allow the purity and power of truth to expose every form of resistance embedded in my conscious or subconscious state of mind, without resistance.

🕉 I intend to bear witness to the truth that uplifts, heals, and strengthens well-being.

🕉 I choose to put my trust in the truth, the creative spirit within me.

🕉 I choose to see the truth of each experience.

🕉 I choose to remember that I Am the way, the truth, and the light.

ॐ I intend to go forth in the truth that I am light and to let my light shine. Because of its presence in me, I can do all things.

ॐ I choose to shine the light of truth of Self on the dark corners of my mind to expose what is dormant, hiding, and ready for transformation.

WELL-BEING

ༀ I choose to stay in the flow of well-being.

ༀ I intend to replace every thought that does not bring well-being.

ༀ I choose to focus on how I would feel if, at this moment, I realized all is well.

ༀ I intend to focus on what I'd love to experience and to express more fully that which enhances my feeling of well-being and joy.

ༀ I intend to choose whatever supports my well-being from moment to moment.

ༀ I choose to merge again with the feeling of connectedness and well-being.

ༀ My intention is always to go where my well-being is encouraged, supported, and amplified.

ༀ I choose to do whatever I do for my well-being, understanding that God is the source of my well-being.

ༀ I choose to imagineer* my well-being as I move from resistance to nonresistance.

ॐ I choose to remember that I have the greatest opportunity in this moment to experience the greatest well-being and the grace of my own Self.

ॐ I choose to focus on how I would feel if I had the solution.

ॐ My intention is to know everything that contributes to my well-being.

ॐ I choose to examine each of my beliefs to see if they support my well-being.

ॐ My primary intention is to uncover my original state of well-being in each moment of mindfulness, wakefulness, and action.

ॐ I choose to focus on what I love doing that allows me to live well.

ॐ I choose to trade in my sense of separateness for a sense of well-being.

ॐ I choose to pay attention at all times to how I feel so that I may adjust my thoughts and experiences to greater well-being.

ॐ I choose well-being with every breath I take, and I will not let anyone rob me of it.

ॐ I choose to surrender to well-being and to the goodness of life.

ॐ I deliberately choose to shift my focus from suffering to images, ideas, qualities, and memories that reconnect me with the stream of pure joy, love, light, and thanksgiving.

ॐ I choose to be in an accelerated program of feeling good, of well-being.

ॐ I choose to flood my consciousness with everything that represents the feeling or state of well-being.

ॐ I intend to express the manifold aspects of love to promote and include my well-being and the well-being of others.

ॐ I choose to continue unfolding intentionally, joyfully, gratefully, and enthusiastically.

ॐ As I exhale, I choose to let go of tension. As I inhale, I choose to allow peace, joy, and well-being to come to me.

ॐ I intend to preserve my feeling of well-being—physically, mentally, emotionally, and physically.

ॐ I choose to manifest everything that enhances well-being by allowing love to lead the way.

ॐ I intend to allow myself enough time to be wherever I need to be so I can enjoy relaxation and well-being beforehand.

ॐ I choose to rejoice in the many ways that God's grace is enhancing my well-being and contributing to my intense desire to experience the divine abundantly and without disruption of conscious awareness.

ॐ I choose to focus on well-being, regardless of what is going on.

ॐ I choose to do only that which makes me feel better.

ॐ I choose to feel better than ever.

ॐ I choose to allow the feeling of well-being to move through all my experiences to ever greater experiences of joy and well-being.

ॐ I choose to connect with as many expressions of well-being as possible from moment to moment.

ॐ I choose to expand the love I feel to include the well-being of all.

ॐ I intend to have 60,000 thoughts of well-being abiding with me every day.

ॐ I intend to catch whatever thought or emotion would undermine my well-being and to shift my focus through intentions and holy vision.

ॐ I choose to grow through inner connectedness and well-being.

ॐ It is my clear, passionate, powerful intention to remain constantly open to all that promotes my well-being, no matter what is happening.

ॐ I choose to reflect on how I can direct any experience to contribute to my well-being.

ॐ I choose to realize divine love provides me with everything I need for my physical, mental, emotional, and spiritual well-being. My cup is overflowing.

ॐ I choose only that which allows me to live in well-being, joy, peace, and creative self-expression.

ॐ When I am not experiencing well-being, I choose to ask: "What feels better than this?"

ॐ I choose to contribute to the well-being of others.

ॐ My intention is to do everything as an offering to my source of well-being. This moves me on the path of least resistance to bliss.

ॐ I choose to dwell only on that which brings feelings of well-being.

ॐ I intend always to look beyond actions to the source of all actions, for this allows me to walk in balance and to be attuned to the stream of pure love, consciousness, and well-being.

*To imagineer means to exercise the limitless creative imagination—supported by magnificent desire and infused with irresistible love—to enliven the subject or object that one intends to realize. Such imagineering involves a state of reverie in which you still the mind by simply breathing consciously and deliberately, enjoying and enlivening the inhalation and exhalation without any intruding thoughts. This happens quite spontaneously. There is the sensation of being uplifted in consciousness and feeling very calm and peaceful. It is in this state of reverie that one proceeds with imagineering, enlivening the image and feeling one's way into it until it assumes a feeling of reality. It is important to enjoy this process, to be playful with it. When concluding it, be sure to give thanks to God, the Image-maker, your creative imagination, and know that when belief, feeling, and imagination are conjoined, success is inevitable.

ABOUT THE AUTHOR

 Sri Swami Shankarananda is a Western Yogi and an illumined Master teaching the universal truth of Vedanta in Baltimore, Maryland, where he established the Divine Life Church of Absolute Oneness. He is a Guru, of the line of Gurus that began with Babaji. His grandfather Guru (Paramguru) is Swami Yogananda Paramhansa, who is well known for his classic book *Autobiography of a Yogi*.

Swami Shankarananda guides the unfoldment of his devotees through established services at the Church, individual spiritual counseling, spiritual hypnotherapy, and the pure example of his own life.

He is a Kriya master, and, as such, he initiates devotees who are ready into the meditation practice of Kriya. A ten-disc CD set has been published entitled *Kriya Yoga: Inner Path to God*.

He has established the Universal Swami Order, which is based on the ancient Swami Order of India, but has been expanded to include women and those who are married as well as unmarried. He is frequently called upon to speak at colleges and other organizations and at spiritual gatherings. He draws upon all the great scriptures of the world and all the spiritual giants to show the universality of truth at the mystical level. His main message is to cultivate unconditional love for all and to live the truths that have been given to humankind.

ABOUT THE EDITOR

 Srimati Shanti Mataji is an ordained minister and Associate Minister of the Divine Life Church in Baltimore. She was consecrated as Mataji by her Guru, Swami Shankarananda. She has been a devotee of Swami's since his days in Washington, DC, and began giving services in Baltimore around 1980.

Her career in the world was largely at the National Geographic Society as a researcher-editor and managing editor. Her own writings include articles for the Church publication as well as a book of poetry entitled *Songs of a Seeking Heart*.

She has two daughters, now grown, and taught Sunday school for many years. She is a Reiki Master and teaches all levels of Reiki to those who wish to participate in this healing art.

She is the founding editor of DARSHAN, a publishing company of Baltimore, Maryland, dedicated to producing books and CDs of the works of Swami Shankarananda.

FOR MORE INFORMATION, PLEASE CONTACT:

DARSHAN

Divine Life Church
5928 Falls Road
Baltimore, MD 21209
e-mail: DivineLifeStore@gmail.com
phone: 410-435-6121

Swami Shankarananda's books and CDs,
including the ten-disc set entitled
Kriya Yoga: Inner Path to God,
are available through our online store
www.DivineLifeChurch.org

1110085R00094

Made in the USA
San Bernardino, CA
16 November 2012